THE

LOST CAUSE REGAINED.

BY EDWARD A. POLLARD

Author of "THE LOST CAUSE," &c.

NEW YORK:
G. W. CARLETON & Co., Publishers.
London: S. LOW, SON & Co.
MDCCCLXVIII.

Stereotype of
Sunnyside Press

"Much ostentation vain of fleshly arm
And fragile arms, much instrument of war,
Long in preparing, soon to nothing brought
Before mine eyes thou hast set; and in my ear
Vented much policy, and projects deep
Of enemies, of aids, battles and leagues,
Plausible to the world, to me worth naught,
Means I must use, thou say'st, prediction else
Will unpredict and fail me of the throne:
My time I told thee (and that time for thee
Were better farthest off) is not yet come;
When that comes, think not thou to find me slack
On my part aught endeavouring, or to need
Thy politic maxims, or that cumbersome
Luggage of war there shown me, argument
Of human weakness rather than of strength
* * * * * * * *

More humane, more heavenly first
By winning words to conquer willing hearts,
And make persuasion do the work of fear.
At least to try and teach the erring soul
Not wilfully misdoing, but unware,
Misled; the stubborn only to subdue."

Milton's "Paradise Regained."

CONTENTS.

—:0:—

PAGE

II.—RECONSTRUCTION.

PAGE

IV.—THE TRUE HOPE OF THE SOUTH.

INTRODUCTION.

The author of the present work wrote a history of the recent war under the title of "The Lost Cause." The fitness of the title was singularly complimented, and the words have since been permanently incorporated in the common language of the people. The author now proposes a title yet more fit and happy for the continuation of his historical work: "The Lost Cause Regained." He does not hesitate to confess that a prolonged and mature reflection has given him larger and perhaps better views of the true nature of the recent war, and especially of its consequences; and he has risen from that reflection profoundly convinced that the true cause fought for in the late war has not been "lost" immeasurably or irrevocably, but is yet in a condition to be "regained" by the South on ultimate issues of the political contest.

It is scarcely possible in any introduction to recite the whole design of a literary work. But the meaning of a title, which perhaps piques curiosity, may be fixed at once in the mind of the reader by the following brief summary of propositions:

That the late war was much misunderstood in the South, and its true inspiration thereby lost or diminished, through the fallacy that Slavery was defended as a property tenure, or as a peculiar institution of labour; when the true ground of defence was as of a barrier against a contention and war of races.

That the greatest value of Slavery was as such a barrier.

That the war has done nothing more than destroy this barrier, and liberate and throw upon the country the ultimate question of the Negro.

That the question of the Negro practically couples or associates a revolutionary design upon the Constitution; and that the true question which the war involved, and which it merely liberated for greater breadth of controversy was the supremacy of the white race, and along with it the preservation of the political traditions of the country.

That in contesting this cause the South is far stronger than in any former contest, and is supplied with new aids and inspirations.

That if she succeeds to the extent of securing the supremacy of the white man, and the traditional liberties of the country —in short, to the extent of defeating the Radical party—she really triumphs in the true cause of the war, with respect to all its fundamental and vital issues.

That this triumph is at the loss only of so many dollars and cents in the property tenure of Slavery—the South still retaining the Negro as a labourer, and keeping him in a condition where his *political* influence is as indifferent as when he was a slave;—and that the pecuniary loss is utterly insignificant, as the price of "the lost cause regained."

These propositions, we believe, sum a novel, and even sublime philosophy on the political questions of the day. They contain the true hope of the South; they suggest a new animation of a contest which lingers too much on mere partial and contracted issues. The great difficulty of the Southern mind is, and always has been, its extreme narrowness on the Negro question. This intellectual defect, in a concern so important and peculiar, is especially remarkable, when we consider what renown the South has obtained for her schools of statesmanship, that she has contributed the largest and best part of the political literature of the country; nevertheless it is a fact. We shall see further on in these pages that the best of Southern statesmen had no clear ideas, either of the nature or the object of the defence of Negro Slavery; that they were incapable of conveying distinct inspirations to the people in the past war, which failed on the side of the South for this reason as well as from material causes; and that in the political controversy which has followed, they have exhibited a pitiful want of due conception of the nature and magnitude of the contest. It is indeed mortifying to witness the present superficiality of the Southern mind, and to read the commentaries of its statesmanship on the political situation. The reigning Radicalism at Washington is lightly treated as a wanton and ephemeral display of party, or, in the most serious mood of the Southern "statesman," is described after the words of Emerson: "the spirit of our American radicalism is destructive and aimless—it is not loving—it has no ultimate ends—but is destructive only out of hatred and selfishness." The common mistake is in regarding as a wanton and aimless excitement, without "ultimate ends," as an extravagant episode of party, what has really the depth and significance of a great revolution—a revolution of unbroken tenour and resolution, proceeding by distinct and firm steps from the time the Anti-Slavery party erected its first starting-post in the theory of Consolidation, and made its first movement upon the Constitution of the United States.

We are living not in the excitement of party, but in the solemnity of a Revolution. We are aware that it has often happened that a people has shown but little cotemporary realization of the events of a Revolution; history is full of pictures of men buying and selling, and perplexed with the paltry cares of every-day life in the midst of great political changes; and it seems indeed to be an unvarying law of the progress of human opinion, that the true proportions of the crisis through which it passes become visible only on retrospect. But in the case we are considering, this popular dullness, especially in the South, is unusually remarkable and excessively curious. The imperfect appreciation of current events, and the degraded estimate of them are so extreme as to claim a particular notice and merit a signal rebuke.

It is to develope the significance of the present revolution in the political affairs of America; to pass in brief review its history; to show its coherent and dramatic design on the twin subjects of Reconstruction and Negrophilism; to deduce from all a new and animating hope for the South, and to point the path to the victory of the Constitution, that we have designed this work.

If we may claim any particular merit for it, it will be found rather in the suggestive than in the exhaustive treatment of the subject. It is not a modest claim we make. We shall consider, indeed, that we have attained some literary excellence, when we have accomplished what is really the superiour office of the writer—to suggest rather than to convey all the thoughts which attach to his subject.

May, 1868.

I.

REVIEW OF THE LATE WAR.

STATESMANSHIP OF THE SOUTH.

A question at the front of the Historical review—How far President Davis' mal-administration was responsible for the results of the War—Lack of a distinct inspiration in the South—Puerilities of Mr. Davis—His first design to take personal command of the armies—How it was defeated—An incident of Manassas—Resignation of Mr. Hunter from the Confederate Cabinet—Richmond, a Chinese copy of Washington—Mr. Seward, the arch-intelligence of the war—European opinions of Mr. Davis and his Administration—A glance at Senator Benjamin—Mr. Davis in the prophet's robe—How he betrayed and lost public confidence—The Emancipation Proclamation not an act of statesmanship—The two notable triumphs of Northern statesmanship—Inattention of the South to the Anti-Slavery measures at Washington—Peculiar crime of Negro enlistments—A reflection on the Confederate finances—Errour of the Impressment law—Analysis of the opposition to Mr. Davis—Mr. Toombs' explanation—Wreck of the Confederate transportation—Private design of Mr. Davis—John M. Daniel's commentary on Yankees—His suspicion of Mr. Davis—Curious mitigation of animosity towards the North—Mr. Stephens' suppression of a proposition from Abraham Lincoln—*Par nobile* of Georgia demagogues—Curious delusion of the South as to the recovery of Slavery—The African Church "revivals"—A remark of Mr. Hughes of Virginia—Historical value of the fact that the South expected generous terms of restoration—What Reconstruction has revealed.

He who justly and intelligently reviews the late war from the eminence of History finds at the front the serious and interesting question:—how far its results are to be ascribed to the relative personal administrations of the two Governments. The author has an opinion, strengthened and assured by time, and of which he will probably never be divested, that the South should have won in the past contest by every rule of historical experience, and according to every method of *a priori* argument, if the administration of her affairs had been good, or even equal to her enemy's; and that she essentially failed for want of a statesmanship competent to energize her resources, and especially to furnish her people a distinct and well-defined inspiration to sustain their arms. The test of such belief is obviously this: that at the time of the surrender of the Confederate armies, the South was still capable of defensive warfare, if there had been a strong popular will to employ all her resources—the want being, not of material, but of animation. There was still population enough to furnish an army of several hundred thousand men; there were accumulations of subsistence, remote and unavailable only through mismanagement, which, by proper exertions, might have been brought into use; there were parts of the country immensely defended by nature, where armies had not yet penetrated; and yet, in direct view of these resources, we find a war tamely expiring, without either of those final experiences almost uniform in history—a last convulsive effort or a resort from the open field to such strong-holds as nature or art have supplied. We know of no other instance in modern history where more than one hundred thousand men have laid down their arms in open fields to an enemy, and have ceased from war with a resolution so sudden and complete.

Those who have known Mr. Davis well—some of them companions of his retreat from Richmond—testify that his last, bitterest thought was that the South was abandoning the war without having exhausted her resources. The unhappy fugitive President saw plainly means to continue the war; but it was the vision of Tantalus. He could not command these means; his power to animate was gone; he could no longer communicate inspiration to the people, and in this moment of anguish—this moral paralysis—he doubtless realized how his misgovernment had squandered public confidence, and how terribly he was repaid. It is said his pale lips writhed and his steps tottered, when, at Abbeville, South Carolina, he made his last appeal to the five brigade commanders left with him, and they received it in such silence as told him there was only a response of pity in their breast. His faculty of inspiration was gone. He might have known it when, two months before this, his speech at the African Church, in Richmond, adopting the Rev. Dr. Burroughs' evangel, that "God had put a hook in Sherman's nose, and was leading him to destruction," fell still-born on the multitude, and was so neglected that but a single newspaper in Richmond reported it, and that only to make it the text of reproof. He might have known it when, fleeing the Confederate capital in a haste so indecent as to leave no souvenir of his departure—not a word of farewell—he published a proclamation at Danville that no one noticed, and that was never even read, after a respectful custom, for the information of the army. If Mr. Davis had not been blinded by vanity, if his eyes had not been sealed by the crudest conceits, he would have realized long before he did, that his power to console and animate the people was utterly gone, and with it every essential and logical hope of the war.

It was, as we believe, on account of a deficiency of statesmanship in the South that the inspiration of the war was completely lost in its last stages, and that it expired with such remarkable tameness. It is notorious that the people of the South never understood exactly for what they were fighting, and that on this subject they received only the most confused instruction from their leaders. Some declared that the contention was for slavery; others that it was for independence; and others again that it was for constitutional liberty, in which the South did nothing more than represent the traditions of the old Government. All these explanations were given at various times, and Mr. Davis exchanged them as convenience served. If, indeed, he had believed (as was his last confession) that the prize was not slavery, but independence and liberty, it would have been severely logical to have sacrificed the former—to have fought the war on the basis of the emancipation of the Negro—and thus have assured one of the most splendid successes of statesmanship that the world has ever seen. But Mr Davis had neither the prescience nor nerve for such a magnificent stroke of genius; and the war suffering for a distinct object necessarily lost that inspiration which was the condition of endurance and the vital element of success.

This, coupled with another notable cause of demoralization, we believe to be the true and profound explanation of the war on the Southern side. The other cause (to be noticed hereafter with some detail) was an undue expectation of generosity from the enemy, that obviously hastened the act of submission, and contributed to the tameness with which that act was ultimately performed. But our present reflection is on that loose conduct of affairs in the South, which not only brought the Administration of Mr. Davis into contempt, which not only gave occasions of personal recrimination, but slowly and sadly reduced the spirit of the people until it sunk to an almost abject submission.

The extreme exhibition of misgovernment which the South made in the contest, and her woeful lack of statesmanship, are curious in consideration of the fact that this part of the country had hitherto been so much renowned for political science. But there is really no inconsistency here. The excellence of the Southern mind was in the abstract science of politics—rather a philosophical accomplishment than a practical virtue. The character of Jefferson Davis illustrates the difference with singular exactness. No man spoke in the United States Senate with greater weight than he on questions of constitutional law and all our political traditions; he was ready and exact in historical illustration; he showed both learning and acumen in debate; he was incontestably one of the best political scholars of his time; and yet, when he came to be President of the Southern Confederacy, it was found that in many matters of practical judgment he was as ignorant as a child, and there might be gathered from his administration a stock of puerilities to amuse the world.

What shall we say of those legislative licences recommended by Mr. Davis, which nearly disbanded the Confederate armies at the conclusion of the first year of the war; of that financial acuteness which, on a particular day, repudiated one third of the currency; of that astute policy which refused to trade cotton for bread and meat, and hugged it to the bosom of the South as the merest stuffing of vanity; of those orders of the commissariat not to bring supplies into the cities, but to leave them in the open country, inviting the enemy's rapacity; of those subscriptions of scrap-iron to build gun-boats, and of silver plate to relieve the distress of the Treasury? In the endeavours of the Government to meet great public necessities there were sometimes exhibitions of stark, innocent puerility almost surpassing belief. John M. Daniel used to laugh over pious Secretary Memminger's idea of replenishing the Treasury by collection bags suspended from poles in the churches; but the expedient was scarcely more trifling than a public call of the Government for the people to cast their jewelry into the Treasury, to assist in the payment of the public debt. What ever became of these contributions we wonder. There were regularly published lists of them to serve as incentives to patriotism; but whether the spoons, butter-dishes, finger-rings, and various baubles of female vanity ever found a market, and for what sort of money, is one of the historical mysteries of the "Lost Cause."

We do not believe it is generally known that in the early part of the war Mr. Davis designed turning over his civil authority to Vice President Stephens, and taking a military command in the field. His first intention was to take personal command of the forces west of the Alleghanies. The advent of General A. S. Johnston, in September 1861, afterwards supplied an able and popular commander for the great western wing of the war. But the chief difficulty that defeated Mr. Davis' intention of taking the field was want of confidence in Alexander H. Stephens as his substitute in the civil administration, and a remarkable backwardness of this person to accept any of the responsibilities of the war.

This political indisposition of Mr. Stephens was afterwards the subject of much remark, and there were many who considered him a masked and suspicious figure in the war. He shunned Richmond; and his proper post of duty as presiding officer of the Senate was constantly filled by substitutes. This dereliction was severely commented upon; and Mr. Stephens' former habits of excessive loquacity were said to have been exchanged for a cold, sullen silence, which he maintained for a long time in his retreat in Georgia. The explanation of his appointment as a commissioner to meet Lincoln and Seward at Fortress Monroe in 1865, was the belief of certain members of Congress that his equivocal character in the war would make him useful as an instrument of pacification, and recommend him to Northern confidence. He was by no means the choice of Mr. Davis for the mission; and when he was imposed upon the President by the pressure of a delegation from Congress, the two were scarcely on speaking terms, and the necessary interview was of the most cavalier description. "I know of no person more fit for the mission," said Mr. Davis as he extended the appointment to Stephens; but as the Confederate President had been very free to say before that it was a shameful, cowardly experiment on Northern sentiment, in which he only sought to satisfy popular clamour, the compliment could scarcely be taken without a perception of its sarcasm. When Mr. Stephens returned, a most earnest effort was made to reanimate the people in view of the results of the mission; delegations and particular persons sought him, entreating him to take part in the famous African Church "revival." "Only speak ten words to let the people know where you are," they pleaded; but Mr. Stephens only replied with a wan smile and a reference to his bodily infirmities, though, despite the latter, he considered himself able to travel over all the ruins of broken railroads and burnt bridges to Georgia, slipping away from Richmond between two days, and avoiding its catastrophe.

We must consider it unfortunate that Mr. Davis did not execute his intention of taking the field, provided his civil authority could have been bestowed upon a worthy person. We have conjectured that his genius (using the word in its low sense of any disposition of mind) was rather military than political; and in any event the country would have had the advantage of an experiment in one direction, where the other was only assured and complete failure. Mr. Davis had throughout the war a remarkable ambition to be considered as the director of its arms rather than its statesman; and hence much of his military pragmatism. It was understood that he would have commanded at Manassas and that he hastened to the field for that purpose, arriving, however, only in time to witness the complete discomfiture of the enemy. Every newspaper in the South had it from the agent of the Associated Press that he "commanded the centre" on that day, and Mr. Davis never contradicted the pleasant report, although returning to Richmond, and speaking from the balcony of the Spotswood House, he gave otherwise detailed and correct information of the engagment.

Of this imperfect military adventure of the ConfederatePresident, there is an incident that should be related to his credit. When he had reached Manassas Junction, and was galloping from the railroad station towards the volume of fire, a swarm of stragglers gave the idea of defeat, he was told that his army was beaten, and some one suggested that he should consult his own personal safety.

"No," replied the President, speaking to his brother, who rode by his side; "if it is so, the greater necessity that we should be at the front and share with our brave fellows the misfortune of the day."

It was a spirited, generous remark, characteristic of Mr. Davis; for whatever his faults, no one ever doubted that he was the most courageous of men, prompt to assume any personal peril—a true son in this respect, of "the soldier State of Mississippi." A few days before this he had promised to lead the Hampton Legion into battle, and, hinting at his intention of taking the field, had declared he would be where "the last line of bayonets was leveled." The war had no such dramatic conclusion; but we believe that Mr. Davis would have been in the foreground and in heroic attitude, if he had persuaded the remnants of the army left him at Abbeville, South Carolina, in April, 1865, to make that last effort which he implored almost to the point of tears.

The first serious wound to public confidence in Mr. Davis' administration was the resignation of Mr. Hunter from his Cabinet. This latter gentleman was by far the most powerful and popular intellect that had been called to the counsel and support of the new administration. He had a national reputation; his rough, seamed face, yet lighted up with splendid eyes, had long been familiar in public life; he had measured his sturdy intellect with the most famous statesmen of his day; he was singularly unostentatious, and yet a man of profound and extensive learning, comprehending accomplishments the most elegant and scholarly. He was an excellent type of the plain, personal figure of the old Virginia politician, united with erudition surprising the casual observer and confounding the critic who ventured upon a flippant treatment of the man who appeared so simple and ordinary. Indeed we know of no living man in the South who yet compares with Mr. Hunter in illustrating the old and honoured race of Southern statesmen. He was placed in Mr. Davis' Cabinet as a compliment to Virginia, and was the only man who brought to it any remarkable reputation.

Memminger was a curiosity—a weak example of the pious statesman; Mallory had not even the dignity of private life to support him, and the name of "the old wharf rat" was suggestive of predatory excursions; Reagan had some ability, but all the faults in coarseness and conceit of "self-educated men," a Texan lawyer who had read Blackstone when he was a wagon-master, spelling out the difficult words by camp-fires and the illumination of pine-knots; Benjamin, who ultimately took Mr. Hunter's place, was facile, a rapid and adroit under-clerk, despatching vast amounts of routine business, but utterly incapable in the higher administration of public affairs. This company was not very pleasant or honourable to Mr. Hunter; but the immediate occasion of his resignation from the Cabinet was a breach with Mr. Davis.

It was in one of the consultations of the Cabinet, just after the battle of Manassas, that Mr. Hunter ventured to express an opinion on the conduct of the war. Mr. Davis turned sharply upon him and remarked: "Mr. Hunter, you are Secretary of State, and when information is wanted of that particular department, it will be time for you to speak." Probably the Confederate President quickly regretted the remark, for he immediately attempted to take the edge off it by a smiling and jocose allusion. But Mr. Hunter showed his resentment on the spot, and the next day sent in his resignation. It was the first advertisement to the public of Mr. Davis' autocratic temper, and his characteristic, fatal disposition to repel, as from a position of rivalry, the company and support of other leading men in the country.

He had, at first, a very servile aid in the Provisional Congress, a miserable creature of "conventions" brought to Richmond from Montgomery, a legislative burlesque. But in the Congresses that succeeded under the "regular" Government, Mr. Davis gradually lost their confidence, and offended the few personal friendships that he had in the legislative body. He did this particularly by refusing his confidence to Congress in the most unprecedented way; and we are assured of the actual fact that he refused, even in secret session, to communicate what had been done in the foreign relations of the Confederacy. He considered the subject of such exclusive, delicate confidence, that he would not have Congress to participate in it; he claimed the field of diplomacy as entirely his own; he sent off the Clay-Thompson commission without Congress knowing a word about it; and the fruits of the diplomacy that affected such severe and grand secrecy were all failures and absurdities without end. In the last periods of the war the President had got to be so entirely without influence, such an obvious failure, that his administration was almost taken out of his hands, unwillingly by Gen. Lee, but readily enough by Congress, which at last assumed the task of negotiation with the enemy, or drove the President, in this respect at least, to be the instrument of its will.

A strong characteristic, running through the whole Government of the Southern Confederacy, and pervading all its legislation, was a feeble but persistent echo to Washington. History will remark this as one of the most curious circumstances of the war. A Government in the position of a seceder, if not of a rebel, was so utterly destitute of statesmanship, so devoid of intellectual force and originality, as to follow with halting and apish imitations upon the Government it had forsaken and denounced. The whole course of Mr. Davis' administration was to borrow examples from Washington, and even to import the men from there to assist in the various departments. Richmond was a Chinese copy of Washington, with all its patches of departments and bureaus, with all its stripes of "red tape," with all its traditions of official circumlocution, with all its ancient stenches of the lobby and back-stairs. We are aware that an attempt has been made to explain this conformity as an ingenious design of Mr. Davis to conciliate public opinion in the North; but the true explanation is intellectual poverty. It is an unquestionable fact that when Mr. Davis commenced the war from the Montgomery Convention, he entertained the hope of the accession of some of the Northern States, and, therefore, the new government was made so exact a copy of the old, tc solicit all possible prejudices in its favour. But when this hope disappeared, as it soon did, what excuse was there, not only for continuing the servile copy to the lowest details in the form of the government, but for conducting the practical administration of all affairs as a low and feeble counterpart to whatever was done in Washington? It is notorious that all the suggestions of legislation in the Provisional Congress, which was easily ruled by Mr. Davis, were borrowed from Washington, and yet reproduced with a faintness that made the imitation contemptible.

The Federal Government multiplied calls for volunteers after the battle of Manassas; the Richmond Congress replied by increasing the Confederate army to "four hundred thousand men," whose only existence was on paper. The Federal Government tried the rigour of confiscations; the echo in Richmond was a "sequestration" law that did not actually produce two milions of dollars. The Federal Government issued immense volumes of paper money; the Richmond Government replied by reckless issues, (Mr. Davis assuring Congress there was not a particle of risk, as the eight per cent bonds would absorb them,) and produced an immitation of the Northern financial system, with the fatal exception that the Treasury notes were not made "legal tenders."

It was a subject of frequent painful remark how basely the Confederate Government followed on the heels of that at Washington. It was a standing subject of reproach in the columns of the Richmond *Examiner*, and the whole intelligence of the South severely but ineffectually resented it. Even the forms of all proceedings in the departments were imported from Washington, and not a single original military text-book was used to any extent in the Southern armies. Mr. Davis was incrusted with the old prejudices he had obtained in the War Office at Washington, and plodded in all the worn routines that had been customary in his former political life. He invented nothing, not even in the least ceremony or detail of the Government, satisfied with a mechanical, barren imitation of what he had learned in Washington.

We shall, hearafter, remark on the relative statesmanship of the North, and shall proceed, after a certain method, to dispose of our subject. But it is not inconvenient here to notice the estimates entertained in the South of the various leading men in the North, and in what proportions were ascribed the statesmanship that directed the war. In this respect Mr. Seward was considered beyond all comparison the arch-intelligence of the war, the man most feared by the people of the South, and hence, perhaps, most abused by them. The names even of the other members of Mr. Lincoln's Cabinet were scarcely known in the South. The Northern President himself was considered only as an instrument in the hands of the wily Secretary of State, who became the impersonation to the people of the South of all the bad wisdom and baffling ingenuities to defeat and plague their cause. Intelligent men in Richmond were very ready to admit that Mr. Seward's vulgar prophecy of a "sixty days' war" was not a sincere conviction of his able mind, but was ingeniously designed to belittle the war in European estimation and to entice volunteers. Thus while the newspapers, for popular effect, ridiculed the prophecy, discerning men were vexed at the success of the game, and saw the ground of "foreign recognition" steadily undermined and cut from under their feet. It is now plain enough that in the single part of preventing European recognition of the Confederacy, Mr. Seward made a contribution to the success of the North far greater than "emancipation proclamations" or any other act of statesmanship, and administered a vital blow to the hopes of the South. The Richmond newspapers always affected to be careless of recognition; but it was a thorough affectation; and to the last Mr. Davis did not cease his anxiety or quit his hopes of interference in some shape from the European powers. There was was an intelligent argument and a strong belief that these Powers had abstained from interference only on conviction that the South was able to accomplish her independence unaided and without complicating them, and that when they were rid of this conviction, and the war had plainly progressed to extremity, they would be prompt to intervene to save a conclusion supposed to be so disastrous to their interests as the recovery of the American Union, with enlarged prestige and power to enforce its demands against the foreign nations and to prosecute its mission against European monarchy. The argument was plausible and captivating; and on the fall of Richmond there was a common report that the sudden conclusion of the war had taken England, and especially France, by surprise, and that the latter was prepared to intervene, had she known the desperation of the case. This belief of a *contretemps* still resides in many minds, and has, for a long time, been a subject of melancholy gossip among those who mourn the defeat of the South.

It is curious what undue and flattering opinions Mr. Davis obtained from European countries, and especially from England.

Those to whom he ever confided his personal feelings testify that he was especially pleased and inflated by this foreign praise, and that he valued it more than the affections of his countrymen. He is said to have written his most ambitious State papers for European effect, and to have taken especial delight in that singular delusion of the English and French journals which long persisted in regarding him as the military hero of the war, the inspirer of campaigns, the Great Captain as well as the civil ruler of the Confederacy—a delusion which he constantly encouraged and absurdly misled in his official references to the conduct of the war. This was not the only mistake of these journals in their distant admiration of Mr. Davis. Impressed by his literary accomplishments, and comparing the decorous and cultivated style of his State papers with the coarse tangled English of Mr. Lincoln, they fell into the not uncommon errour of accepting as a profound statesman a man who was only an elegant scholar.

This European misjudgment of Mr. Davis sometimes proceeded to absurdities of praise, which were curious and amusing, when read in Richmond. People who had a close and interiour view of the slattern government of the Confederacy were surprised to find it represented abroad as a model of energy, and Mr. Davis raised to a historical figure comparable with Cromwell, Garibaldi and such famous leaders of revolutions. It was common, too, in this European estimate, to represent him as surrounded by the most skilled statesmen of the South, in face of the fact that his Cabinet of dummies was one of the greatest curiosities of the war and that the Confederate President was peculiar among rulers for constantly repelling from his counsels all men of any note in the country, and choosing an eminence as naked as possible. As an evidence of this excess of eulogy, the author recollects to have copied the following from one of the British Quarterlies, with reference to the least deserving member of Mr. Davis' Cabinet:—" Mr. Benjamin is not one of those grave, weighty, and self-contained natures which, when illuminated by brightness of intellect, never fail to impress their work deeply on all around them. Easily accessible, voluble, good-natured, with a memory like Macaulay's, and singular grace and facility of expression, Mr. Benjamin has failed to win from his countrymen, and especially from the journalists of Richmond, one tithe of the respect and admiration which they who know him best conceive to be his due. As a speaker, though not as a statesman, he has probably, since the death of Webster, had no equal in the old United States Senate! "

If such was Mr. Benjamin's fame in the "old United States Senate," he greatly descended from it in Richmond, where in point of abilities, he was known only as an expert subordinate, a dapper under-clerk in the sinecure of Confederate diplomacy. He was Secretary of the War Department for some time, but was driven from it for his excessive freedom in granting passports through the military lines, especially to the Jews who flocked in wonderful numbers from all points of the compass to the official patronage of one of their own religion in so high a place of government. Like all the other members of Mr. Davis' Cabinet, Mr. Benjamin did only the duties of a clerk, exerted no political influence, and made no impression whatever on the war. No one ever heard in Richmond of a Cabinet-meeting in the usual sense of a political council, or of the heads of the Departments having any peculiar ideas of the war. This negative character of Mr. Davis' Cabinet was fully known in the South; and it may be remarked, in passing, that any attempt to excuse his mal-administration is singularly baffled by this fact, and that it is but just to make his autocracy the measure of his responsibility.

If statesmanship is to be regarded as prescience, then Mr. Davis had least of this gift. He went about at all times of the war, frequently in the unnecessary character of a public speaker, prophesying the speedy and easy accomplishment of Southern Independence. He commenced these announcements as early as 1862, when in a speech in Mississippi, he declared in his rhetorical way, that the evening of peace was already spreading its mild radiance on the horizon. Some of these prophetic words, so often renewed and re-dated, are very curious. They are evidences of such puerility of mind, of such levity and insolence and ignorance all combined, that future sober history will be perplexed to account for them. As an instance we may take Mr. Davis' "Address to the Soldiers" in the last year of the war, made on a most elevated occasion and intended to inspire them against those grand campaigns of Grant and Sherman which were already being prepared on the borders of Virginia and Georgia. It is well known that this year was that of supreme, most elaborate trial on the part of the North; the vastest materials were accumulated; the Federal armies were greatly increased; tens of thousands of men were brought out by additional drafts, or lashed into the fields by golden thongs of bounties; all along the front of the war was spread the busy and effulgent preparation. In the face of this imposing display of the enemy, what shall we say of this silly speech of the Confederate President: "The enemy's campaign of 1864 must, from the *exhaustion of his resources* of men and money, be far *less formidable* than those of the last two years, when unimpaired means were used with boundless prodigality, and with results which are suggested by the mention of the names of Shiloh, Perryville, Murfreesboro, and the Chickahominy, Manassas, Fredericksburg and Chancellorsville!"

These flippant prophecies of speedy success were doubtless intended to animate the South. But in this respect it was the thought of a small mind, a shallow trick; and it had the fault, too, of being calculated without reference to a peculiar temper of the Southern people in the war. That temper was one of impatience, almost of mutiny, under peculiar hardships; and thoughtful men remarked it more than once in the exhibitions of the war. It grew out of the very elements of Southern society. Here was a people of singularly high spirit, who had enjoyed a previous prosperity perhaps greater than that of any other community of equal numbers on earth, who had lived, although perhaps sometimes without cultivation, yet always in ease, and who had their due share of republican indisposition to submit to severe exercises of authority. A people so sensitive should have been lightly taxed with disappointments, and the policy of amusing them with promises was essentially a delicate and dangerous one. It would have been the task of a true statesman to have moderated their expectations, and to have educated them to just conceptions of the trials of the war. Instead of such prudent cultivations of strength, Mr. Davis went to the opposite extreme of inflaming the army and people with promises, and while foolishly congratulating himself on the momentary excitements that flared out under such appeals, he did not perceive that the heart of the country was being steadily consumed by this policy and that with each false appeal to public confidence he lessened his hold upon it. He was at last, however, to see that hold utterly broken and despised and to find no other response to those promises, with which he had formerly kindled public spirit than contempt or pity for him as a deluded man. His last promise ventured a few weeks before the evacuation of Richmond, was "that before the summer solstice of 1865 the South would be dictating terms of peace"; but that solstice found him a lone prisoner who had been degraded by fetters, within the walls of Fortress Monroe!

In a former paragraph we made a slight reference to the statesmanship of the North, and suggested a comparison in this respect between the Government at Washington and at Richmond. Referring again to this subject we have to correct an errour that has very extensively prevailed in the North. This errour is that the Anti-Slavery measures of Mr. Lincoln's Administration were great elements of statesmanship, and that they exerted considerable influence to terminate the war, and secure the success of the North. These laws in this respect have been most unduly valued by a party in the North. They were properly notable triumphs of partisanship; but they were certainly not acts of statesmanship, and their influence was, indeed, utterly inconsiderable in affecting the mind of the South, one way or the other, and determining the practical course of the war.

The true points of statesmanship on which the North triumphed were two: the prevention of European interference and the wonderful success of the Federal finances. The great and even prime anxiety of the South was directed to the financial question and its most intelligent hope of success looked constantly and eagerly to the breaking down of the finances at Washington, since it was argued that this would have the double effect of diminishing the means of war and of turning public attention in the North to an internal concern and breaking it up into new parties. In the Richmond journals it was usual to put the gold quotations at the head of Northern news, as the most important item of intelligence. Mr. Davis appears to have appreciated the importance of this topic, and to have shared the common popular anxiety for the latest financial news from the North. But we may judge how small and narrow were his views on this subject, when we learn that he hoped to break down the Federal finances by withholding cotton, and actually gave this as his reason against certain propositions, to trade cotton through the lines for meat and bread for the army. It was shown to him that if he accepted these propositions, so wide-spread was the venality of the enemy, he might trade at various points in the Mississippi Valley for supplies to support the Confederate armies for years to come. But with his singular fatality to delusion he rejected a scheme of such vital benefits, because he was persuaded that without cotton to export, the Washington Government would be unable to pay the January interest of 1863 on its bonds! This sage opinion we have in black and white from Mr. Davis' hand; else such a display of contraction and credulity of judgment might well be doubted.

While foreign relations and finances were thus the leading cares of statesmanship in the war, the Anti-Slavery measures at Washington fell upon the South almost without attention. From the commencement of the war the South had assured itself of the enemy's design to free the slaves; it suffered no surprise or shock in this respect; and as the Federals had already practically freed the Negroes within their military lines, the Emancipation Proclamation did not really amount to any difference in the estimation of the Southern people, or give them any new cause of alarm. It excited no political interest whatever. Mr. Davis referred to it in a few historical phrases in one of his messages; and ninety-eight clergymen in the South signed "an address to Christians throughout the world" unmasking the hypocrisy of the measure, and indicating its immorality.

The moral interest of the Emancipation Proclamation was, indeed, quite apart from any regard for it as a State paper; and on this aspect of the question, the Southern journals made repeated and lively commentaries. The point was to show that the measure did not really originate out of benevolence for the Negro, that it was a false pretence in this respect; and for this, evidences, mostly derived from Northern sources, were constantly accumulated. The writer recollects to have published in a Richmond paper, with great effect, the following yet memorable statement of Rev. Mr. Fiske, an army chaplain:—

"Out of an average number of 4,000 blacks under my charge at Memphis during the months of February, March, and April, 1863, there died during that time 1200. Three-fourths of them had no change of raiment; probably one-fourth of the women had but one garment between them and utter nakedness. Many children were kept, night and day, rolled in the poor blanket of a family—its sole apparel. Multitudes had no beds. There were no floors in their leaky tents, and no chance for fires. The wonder is not that so many died, but that so many lived. The suffering of this people is our national dishonour. If they are not rescued, History will run thus:—'The American people enticed within their lines tens of thousands of slaves, alluring them with promises of liberty. They proceeded to pick out all the able-bodied men, to re-inforce their armies, huddled the rest together in great camps, and left them to perish of hunger and nakedness, by the hundred!'"

It is precisely thus that History *does* run. There is an interest of the late war yet undeveloped in the crime done the Negro under the professions of Emancipation, and especially in the price of liberty extorted from him in military service. He was driven into the army by rhetorical flourishes. In a contribution to a literary periodical the author has taken occasion thus to comment on the use of the Negro by the North: "There are some pages of the history of the past war yet unwritten, wherein, some day, will be justly described the cruel and inhuman use of the Negro as a soldier, of which Mr. Wilson of Massachusetts was one of the legislative instruments. He was regarded only as 'food for powder'; he was substituted for the recreant white patriotism of the North; he was driven to slaughter where white troops refused to go; he was made a shield for their cowardice, and used throughout the war as a contemned ally and stipendiary, always bearing an undue share of its burdens and dangers. This is historical fact. Precisely the same use that was made of them as military allies is now designed of them as political followers. Their employment is to be one of subserviency, by which white politicians of the Wilson stamp are to ascend and profit. He is one of that Radical council at Washington which has lately been advising the Negroes most illogically, not to elect men of their own colour to office, but to help the wandering carpet-bag men of New England to fame and profit. He has no sentiment or mania about the son of Ham; he finds him a convenient creature, a useful ally, a serviceable yoke-fellow in certain places, but in no sense an equal and fraternal companion. Of all hypocrisies of these political times, this is the blackest and cruellest. It would work the Negro to the bone in its own selfish service; pat him, and pet him, and palter with him, and eventually leave him to die on the dunghill. Despite all the affectations of Radicalism, the fact is beyond dispute and of daily growth and obviousness that there is a great, crying want of a large, adequate, intelligent benevolence for the Negro. The Radical party does not supply this want; no political organization does; and we shall probably not see one of the greatest problems of modern times practically solved until there shall arise some scheme of benevolence for the Negro, wholly apart from political parties, and much more deeply founded in humanity."

We return to the rival statesmanship of the parties to the war. While the unbroken finances of the North enabled it to keep immense armies in the field, and to spread a factitious prosperity through the country, the utter failure of the Confederate currency did more perhaps to demoralize the war than any other single cause, and hurried the final catastrophe. It must be admitted in the comparison that there were peculiar difficulties attending the financial system of the Confederacy, especially those growing out of the isolation of the blockade. Capital in the South was at first freely and generously invested in the Confederate bonds; but there was a peculiar limit to this aid. It was drawn principally from banks, from merchants driven out of business, and from trust estates and charitable institutions. Such sources were limited and soon exhausted; and nothing remained but to flood the country with paper money. The evils of a depreciated currency are of the most various description; they pervade all the channels of public life and are felt in every daily care of the people. In the South they produced universal distress and penetrated every home; they were named as the prime cause of desertion from the army; and they at last forced the Government to that unpopular measure of "impressment" which ultimately recoiled upon it, and furnished a powerful argument to an opposition party that was fast becoming formidable.

It should be noticed that in the Confederacy was a party

somewhat analogous to that which, in Washington, admitting the legitimacy of the war and professing a desire for its success, was yet constantly interposing objections to assumptions of unconstitutional power. In the Confederacy, however, this party of opposition was singularly pure and enlightened; its sincerity was above suspicion; and so far from opposing the errours of Mr. Davis' Administration factiously, it did so only because these errours were bringing the Confederate cause into hatred and contempt. Its spirit is well illustrated in the passage of a speech of one of its most elevated leaders—Mr. Toombs of Georgia—opposing the Impressment law. "I have," said Mr. Toombs, speaking in November, 1863, "heard it frequently stated, and it has been maintained in some of the newspapers in Richmond, that we should not sacrifice liberty to independence; but I tell you, my countrymen, the two are inseparable. If we lose our liberty we shall lose our independence; and when our Congress determined to support our armies by impressment, gathering supplies wherever they found them most convenient, and forcing them from those from whom their agents might choose to take them, in violation of the fundamental principles of our Constitution, which requires all burdens to be uniform and just, and paying for them such prices as they choose, they made a fatal blunder which cannot be persisted in, without endangering our cause, and probably working ruin to our Government." Yet Mr. Toombs although thus protesting against an unconstitutional resource was zealous for every act of devotion and sacrifice to the war, without the pressure of violent and unequal laws; there was no more ardent Southern patriot; and in the same speech from which we have quoted, referring to the enemy's hope of subjugation, he said, "I would rather see this whole country the cemetery of freemen than the habitation of slaves."

The results of Impressment were meagre, and by no means repaid the hostility it caused the Government. In vain Mr. Davis appealed to the generosity of the people, and said, with his usual extravagance, in April, 1863, that there was "*but one* danger, the failure of provisions." There were many other dangers; and even when supplies were accumulated, they rotted in the depôts, for want of transportation. The railroads that were available were few; and, indeed, when these modes of transportation are in the best condition, it is an enormous task to convey on a single line all that is requisite for a great army. In Virginia, the railroads were already so worn and of such little worth, that speed on them was reduced to ten miles an hour, and tonnage from twenty-five to fifty per cent. The scarcity of food, the wreck of transportation, and other material difficulties and hardships added to a general distress in the South already multiplied by the extreme unpopularity of Mr. Davis' political measures. The fact is the Southern people had no true idea of the trials to which they were to be subjected, until the fall of Fort Donelson in the West and the simultaneous commencement of McClellan's advance on Richmond in the East unveiled the extended front of the war, and revealed the magnitude of the task which still lay before them. But it was too late then, in the second year of hostilities, to repair many fatal omissions; to send the cotton out of the country, to obtain a basis for the currency, to import large stocks of supplies. And so from this period of sober afterthought, the South may be said to have lost its former perfect and almost insolent confidence in the war and to have lived in a feverish anxiety varying with the fortunes of its arms, at one time mounting to hope, and again sinking to depths of despondency and discontent.

The last desperate attempt of the Confederate Government to re-animate the war and inflame anew the resentment of the people was on the occasion of the famous Fortress Monroe commission. In the minds of some leading persons in the South, the interview with President Lincoln and Mr. Seward was a sincere experiment on the sentiment and temper of the Northern Government; but Mr. Davis had consented to it with the especial view of obtaining an ultimatum from the enemy so harsh as to exasperate the people of the South, and to put before them a plain alternative, which he calculated would be a continuation of the war, or an unconditional submission too absolute to be entertained. The secret thought in Richmond of the Fortress Monroe commission was thus, strangely enough, to kill off the "peace conferences" rather than to improve the growing tendency to negotiation. In some respects Mr. Davis calculated aright; but the scheme of re-animation utterly failed for peculiar reasons, and the speeches at the African Church on the choice of "liberty or death" were the most inglorious fizzles of an expiring contest.

The official report of the Confederate Commissioners was carefully prepared, so as to exclude all hopes of further negotiations for peace, and to summon the South to new and desperate resolution; it was a very scant document, and made the impression that the interview with the Federal representatives was singularly harsh and formal. But, unfortunately for the object of Mr. Davis, there leaked out some private versions of the conference which showed the official report to be partial and sinister, and suggested a friendly and generous disposition of President Lincoln quite at variance with the spirit in which he was officially represented to have replied to the Commissioners.

In private accounts of the conference, Mr. Seward was especially represented as kindly, and very much disposed to enter into a general amicable conversation with the Confederate Commissioners. He asked Mr. Hunter with amiable solicitude of many of those they had mutually known in former days in Washington, and inquired particularly of the health of Mr. Davis. There were no marks of harshness in the conference, and no attendance of ceremonies and forms. At parting Mr. Seward shook Mr. Hunter by the hand very warmly, and said, with effusion, "God bless you, Hunter!"

The author recollects to have made some reference to this and other incidents of personal amiability in this famous conference, and to have designed publishing it in the Richmond *Examiner*; but Mr. Daniel ruled it out sharply, and for a special reason. He always forbade the publication of any of the amenities of the war; he thought they were likely to mislead as to the true character and conduct of the enemy, and to soften the resolution of the South. It was necessary, he thought, to paint the Yankee very black and to introduce him constantly in circumstances of atrocity; and the excursions and whiskey bouts under flags of truce, and all amiable episodes of the war was the peculiar detestation of the *Examiner*. Mr. Daniel was naturally atrabilious, a dark fierce man with a hard, electric glitter in his eyes; satire and invective were the habits of his genius; but he had a hatred of the Yankee that was positively savage. Once he said, "sentimentalism is as much out of place in destroying Yankees, as in *killing chinches!*"

He had an inveterate complaint against Mr. Davis for his

apparent tenderness in abstaining from retaliation for the numerous murders committed by the enemy outside the pale of war; but it is fair to say that he did not altogether attribute the hesitation of the Confederate President compel to justice in these cases to a false sentimentalism, although that was commonly supposed to be a weakness of his character. He had a deeper explanation for it in his private conversations. On his intimate friends he repeatedly urged the idea that Mr. Davis was studious to extricate himself from all personal consequences in case of failure of the war, that he carefully provided for his own safety in such event, and that he therefore feared to exact any retribution from the public enemy, for which he might hereafter be called personally to account. Whatever the value of this opinion, it is a little curious that in not one single case Mr. Davis ever took life on the plea of retaliation, although he published numerous orders to that effect (as in the case of the Palmyra Massacre). He always recoiled at the last moment, and the backward movement was sometimes so plain as to excite such explanations as Mr. Daniel has given.

In the last stages of the war, and contributing to its termination, there was a marked decline of hostility to the Yankee, a softening of that fierce animosity which the newspapers had cultivated as a stimulant in the contest. The wonder is that this should have been so, when the outrages of Sherman were fresh, and when the enemy was really in his fiercest and most destructive moods, and the atrocity of his arms at its height. The explanation is very peculiar, and one must have closely studied public sentiment in the South to understand its curious condition on this particular subject towards the end of the war. It was an effect produced entirely by politicians who had had frequent opportunities in various conferences, regular or irregular, with Northern men to inform and mitigate public opinion as to the real designs of the enemy. The idea was spread, sometimes insidiously, that although the North was violent in the war, its excesses in this might be forgiven, as proceeding not so much from cruelty as from a false notion of military necessity, and that its political design was really of the most moderate and indifferent description, meaning only the re-establishment of the Union, and the restoration of the *status quo* in every other particular. The reports brought back from the conferences referred to were generally those of the most polite and pleasant personal intercourse, of hearty fellowship and kind entertainment on the enemy's part. Many of the politicians who had enjoyed such interviews, or who had Northern correspondence, had heard in a confused way of the most liberal propositions, and were ready to assure their weary countrymen of almost any terms of peace, on the single condition of laying down their arms, and trusting themselves to the generosity of the North.

Under these representations, generally made privately and insidiously, and never venturing in the columns of the press, where the death's head of "Subjugation" was constantly displayed, the idea grew in the Southern mind that the Yankee was not such a terrible monster after all, that the newspapers had been practising scare-crows on the people, and that the government had only for its own selfish purposes exaggerated the demands of the enemy and painted the terrours of submission. The extent of this delusion in the last days of the Confederacy can scarcely be conceived by one not admitted to those under-currents of opinion which make the secret history of governments in great wars. It was a whispered thought, an adroit suggestion, rather than a declared idea making its appearance in the press, or circulated in open debate. While the newspapers displayed the horrours of submission, and John Mitchel wrote in serial articles the parallel between Ireland and the conquered South, and President Davis continued the stereotype of "death preferable to defeat," the idea went secretly and steadily abroad in the South that the Yankee was not as black as he was painted, and that surrender was not the chief of evils.

Of this delusion towards the end of the war (so inconsistent with the public tone of the South and especially with the defiance of Mr. Davis) the author ventures to make this curious remark: that many men in the South were even led to doubt of the loss of Slavery in the final adjustment with the enemy, and on this particular account were induced to relinquish the contest. This supposition may appear very extravagant at this day; but it should be remembered that at the time referred to, the South had very imperfect communications with the North, that she was a prey to rumours, and that politicians were busy with the story of the generous temper of the enemy. People were told in whispered conversations that it was not impossible that, at some time after the surrender of their arms, Slavery might be recovered from the yielding disposition of the North; a second supposition was yet more probable, to the effect that they might expect pecuniary compensation, if they promptly and gracefully accepted emancipation, and rumours were already flying in the air that President Lincoln had intimated such a proposition to Alexander H. Stephens in the conference at Fortress Monroe.

Mr. Stephens has since confessed (if we are to believe a Georgia newspaper) that in that conference Mr. Lincoln said to him:

"Your people might after all get four hundred thousand dollars for the slaves, and you would be surprised if I should call the names of some of those who favour such a proposition." But this important disclosure has been so severely suppressed since the death of Mr. Lincoln, as an injury to his memory in Northern estimation, that the public even to this day is scarcely aware of it, or is unprepared to credit it. Certainly, it would have been more manly for Mr. Stephens to have made this disclosure in his public report of the conference, instead of submitting the bald statement he did and locking in his breast so important a secret.

The difficulty of Mr. Stephens was that of duplicity, a common vice of politicians, and of which the South had some very painful illustrations in the war. Probably at this time Mr. Stephens was really solicitous for negotiation with the enemy, and disposed to make a clean breast of the Fortress Monroe affair, an honest disclosure of all he knew. But he was estopped by his former excessive speeches, in which in a more hopeful period of the war he had courted public favour by denouncing a reconstruction of the Union as the sum of all shame, the completion at once of the ruin and disgrace of the South. There must have stuck in his memory some of the words he had used in a speech in North Carolina in the year 1863. Then he said: "Subjugation would be utter ruin and eternal death to the Southern people, and all that they hold most dear. Rather than submit to anything short of final and complete separation from the North, let us all resolve to die like men worthy of freemen." Such was the language of the man who subsequently went on the errand of Fortress Monroe, to inquire the terms of re-admission into the Union, and then took refuge in a fraudulent version of the interview.

It is remarkable that of the most conspicuous men in the Confederacy who coquetted for peace in 1864, they were those who in former periods of the war had been most severe and savage in denouncing any effort towards reunion with the North, even in the last extremity. So another Georgia politician, a competitor of Mr. Stephens in the games of popularity —Herschel V. Johnson—was busy in 1864 with a scheme of a convention of all the States to restore the Union; yet this same man in the preceding year thus glowed in a public harrangue:—" The bleaching bones of one hundred thousand gallant soldiers, slain in battle, would be clothed in tongues of fire to swear to everlasting infamy the man who whispers 'yield.'" Something, to be sure, may be pardoned to the zeal and inflation of the popular declaimer; and something must be allowed for modifications of opinion by the varying fortunes of the Confederate arms; but changes of sentiment so excessive as those we have noted are essentially the evidences of heartless demagogues, and should be remembered to condemn them forever in the estimation of the honest and humane.

The author would occupy too much space, if he was to cite even the leading examples within his knowledge of displays of Southern demagogues touching peace negotiations within the last two years of the war. He returns to the history of public sentiment on that subject. As far back as the last months of the year 1863, a popular sentiment had commenced in North Carolina looking to negotiations with the North, and prepared to accept the restoration of the Union. The sentiment was timid, and not disposed to court discussion. It first grew out of a distrust of the military fortunes of the South; but it was wonderfully increased, as we have already noticed in the last year of the war, by milder regards of the enemy and the remarkable delusion that there might be obtained from him terms of generosity, even embracing the fallen fortunes of Slavery. Many persons will be skeptical of the existence of such a hypothesis in the popular mind of the South, because it was unperceived by them, or because the experience of the present renders it absurd.

Those, however, are imperfect tests. President Davis appears to have been made aware, some months before the close of the war, of the existence of such a hope in the Southern mind, and he considered it so dangerous to the Confederate cause, so well calculated to diminish its energies in the war, that he made special endeavours to expel it. He referred particularly to it in a speech at Augusta, Georgia, in October, 1864. "Some there are," he said, "who speak of Reconstruction with slavery maintained; but are there any who would thus measure rights by property!—God forbid." He continued to explain that the South was not in a revolution, that it was fighting for "constitutional liberty," and he exhorted his audience that the stake was not only Slavery but every right, interest and hope attached to liberty and summed in the existence of freemen.

These exhortations were made for the last time on the return of the Confederate Commissioners from Fortress Monroe; and they were made ineffectually. It is curious to notice how the especial purpose of re-animating the war was served in that famous meeting at the African Church, to accomodate which all business was suspended in Richmond, and a day taken for public orations. Mr. Hunter, one of the Commissioners, addressed the multitude, and gave them to understand that Mr. Lincoln had turned from the propositions of peace with cold insolence—an insolence which he described as monstrous, since the Federal President "might have offered something to a people with two hundred thousand soldiers, and such soldiers under arms." The frightful apparition of Subjugation was next indroduced. "I will not attempt," said Mr. Hunter, "to draw a picture of Subjugation. It would require a pencil dipped in blood to paint its gloom." Mr. Benjamin, Secretary of State, followed with yet more artful appeals to the multitude. He affected to witness the animation which he designed to produce, and spoke of it with exciting praises. "How great the difference in one short week! It seems an age, so magical has been the change! Hope beams in every countenance! We now know in our hearts that this people must conquer its freedom or die!" The Confederate Congress continued the same adroit style of taking for granted a change of popular sentiment. In an address to the people, it declared: "Thanks be to God, who controls and overrules the counsels of men, the haughty insolence of our enemies which they hoped would intimidate and break the spirit of our people is producing the very contrary effect."

The effect of these rhetorical stimulants could scarcely have been less than some momentary excitement; but after all that was publicly said, the thought still resided in the public mind that the Richmond Government was dealing unfairly with it, and that the enemy was not as inaccessible or as harsh as he was represented. This opinion progressed to the day of the surrender. It was this peculiar trust in the generosity of the North, this mollification of hatred of the Yankee and of the passions with which the war commenced, coupled with an entire want of confidence in the Davis Administration and a certain resentment towards it, that brought the Southern Confederacy to such a sudden and almost abrupt conclusion of the war. The author is very firm in this conviction, and is prepared to defend it against all proper and seasonable criticism. The popular mind of the South, all official protestations to the contrary, expected a generous treatment after the war, and had lost its faith in the conventional terrours of Subjugation, so long maintained in the newspapers and in the public demonstrations of the Richmond Government. As evidence of this disposition, the people of the South accepted the famous Johnson-Sherman Convention, as a natural event; there were no transports of surprise when it was first announced to the people of the South; they considered it only as the declaration of the *status quo*, in which they were to resume their equal and accustomed places in the Union, as they expected when they had laid down their arms. This was the common thought in the act of surrender, and which, indeed, hastened the termination of the war. It was not disturbed until the Northern Congress commenced its "problem of Reconstruction," awoke the people of the South from their delusions and confirmed the worst prophecies of Subjugation to which they had sealed their ears in the last periods of the war.

A few weeks before Lee's surrender, one of the most accomplished and thoughtful men in the South (Robert W. Hughes, of Virginia,) said to the author: "The war will fail because the people of the South never had to the time of taking up arms that actual experience of hardship and oppression sufficient to justify a rebellion, and calculated to furnish moral animation enough to sustain it."

It has been curiously reserved for the South to obtain *after* the war the actual experience of oppression, and of that measure of despotism which would have amply justified the commencement of hostilities. If it fought, in 1860, for principles too abstract, it has superabundant causes for rebellion now, which although they may not, and need not produce another war, yet have the effect to justify, in a remarkable way, the first appeal to arms. It is a justification on retrospect, but none the less striking on that account. The author has been particular to describe that delusive faith in Northern moderation, that reaction from the first passions of the war which hastened the submission of the South, and made it an easy descent from her original aspiration of independence, because he believes that this discovery of motive is one of great historical importance and furnishes some very interesting reflections on the present political situation at Washington. Those reflections he may pursue in another chapter. It is sufficient to conclude here that the South has been the victim of delusive hopes, and that she abandoned the war, not so much under the compulsion of military necessities, as from the persuasions of a false political hypothesis.

I

RECONSTRUCTION.

THE DESTRUCTION OF THE WAR.

Realization of its losses in the South—Political "vivisection"—The material civilization of the North, the conqueror—Its characteristic warfare—A curious reminiscence of B. F. Butler—The "problem" of Reconstruction—President Lincoln in Richmond—Afterthought of the Republican party.

The sun of another Austerlitz rose in Virginia. The green banners of the spring of 1865 hung thick about the Capitol mound in Richmond, when a hundred cannon on the brow of that historic hill celebrated the surrender of Lee's Army, and thundered the message of peace. There was then discovered by the people of the South what had hitherto been put behind convenient curtains by their rulers, or been concealed by ornaments of their own vanity and hopes—the vast ruin of the war; the pool of blood and the withered corpses around it; the back-ground with its piles of dead and monuments of woe. The illuminated curtain was drawn up; the atmosphere of glory was darkened and subdued, the garish lights turned down, and realized for the first time by the people of the South was the wan picture of the ruins of their country. The embroidery of war, the cloth of gold was lifted—and the stark corpse was beneath it, the chilled flesh and the dumb wounds—

"Woe to the hand that shed this costly blood!
Over the wounds do now I prophesy—
Which, like dumb mouths, do ope their ruby lips,
To beg the voice and utterance of my tongue—
A curse shall light upon the limbs of men;
Domestic fury and fierce civil strife
Shall cumber all the parts of Italy."

As long as the war was active, and the South possessed the animation of glory and the inspiration of her passions, there was no count of the cost, and but little realization of losses. The Government suppressed the details of disasters; the press was vain and effulgent to the last. But with the end of the war came the discovery and calculation of its losses.

Its total sum was the most enormous of modern convulsions. It has been calculated thus: three thousand millions of dollars lost in the slaves, two thousand millions in ravages of the country and acts of destruction, and, at least, two thousand millions more in the sacrifices of credits and in the depreciation of property consequent upon the war—seven thousand millions in all!* Of all this wealth the South was disemboweled by the sword—so much cut out of her vitals; and the danger was that of utter collapse in the shrunken body politic, death of a community from which had been carved so much of flesh and blood. We have heard of those terrible medical dissections—*vivisections* they are called—which experiment upon animal

* The losses of the South in the war have recently been stated at a larger figure. The following estimate of them is from a late speech of Senator Doolittle—one of the most moderate and judicious members of the United States Senate:—"The people of the South have been punished already by the sacrifice of all their slave property, valued at three to four thousand million dollars; by the sacrifice of more than three-fourths of all other personal property, probably two thousand millions more; by the sacrifice of their public and private credits—at least a thousand millions more; by the depreciation of the value of all their real estate at least seventy-five per cent—amounting probably to more than two thousand million dollars more—making in all a sacrifice of property, credits, and values in the Southern States alone of at least nine thousand million dollars."

existence, and see what parts can be taken from the body, and yet leave an imperfect, hideous life. The South lived after the operation, survived the loss and torture; but surely the penalty was enough, and devils only might have thought of taking further vengeance upon the torn and mutilated victim.

The exhibition of the past war was a conflict of two schools of opinion, long contestant but most unequally supplied with physical instruments and resources. It was a profound and long-continued conflict between the political and social systems of North and South, with which Negro Slavery had a conspicuous connection; a conflict on which was ranged on one side the party that professed the doctrines of consolidation and numerical majorities; that represented the material civilization of America; that had the commerce and the manufactures, the ships, the workshops, the war-material of the country—on the other side the party that maintained the doctrines of State-rights, studied government as a system of checks and balances, and cultivated the highest schools of statesmanship in America; that represented a civilization scanty in shows and luxuries, but infinitely superiour in the moral and sentimental elements; that devoted itself to agriculture, and had nothing but its fields and brave men to oppose to a people that whitened every sea with their commerce, and by the power of their wealth, and under the license of "legitimacy," put the whole world under tribute for troops and munitions.*

In this unequal match of force, aggravated, as we have seen, by a disproportion of statesmanship and other causes,

* And yet notwithstanding this inequality of material resources, a recent New York *Herald* (of March 21, 1868) describes the past war as "an attempt that came nearer success than ever did such revolt before!"

the material civilization of the North conquered, and impressed itself upon the entire history of the struggle. It originated a coarse characteristic warfare, destitute of those ingenious methods and fine emotions, which have made of modern war an intellectual game and a moral inspiration, and thus dignified and adorned it—a cruel mechanical warfare of numbers and *vis anertie*, disdaining all sentimentalism, and justifying all means that might most certainly accomplish the end of subjugation. It was a war which ravaged the country, not to disable the enemy, but to "strike terrour" into the general population; which spared no age, sex, or condition; which burnt two thousand churches; which sacked the homes of the helpless and afflicted; which violated every humanity, and brought before the startled attention of the civilized world the picture of a conflict devoided of all the heroic and chivalric sentiments which were thought to attend modern arms, and repeating some of the worst atrocities of a past and barbarous age.

When Gen. Benjamin F. Butler marched into Maryland in the first year of the war, at the head of Massachusetts troops, he issued an order to his command that "any unauthorized interference with private property will be most signally punished." He only wished to march to Washington, "peaceably, quietly, and civilly, in obedience to the request of the President." He tendered to Governor Hicks the assistance of his troops to suppress a threatened servile insurrection. When Governor Andrew of Massachusetts ventured to reprove him for this act as one of "unmerited grace," Butler replied: "It was simply a question of good faith and honesty of purpose." He declared that to use the Negro in the war would be to repeat that *legend of infamy* in the Revolution, when the British ministry, in availing themselves of the alliance of the red man, asked, "May we not use all the means which God and nature have put into our hands to subjugate the colonies?"—and growing warmer in the argument, he proceeded to declare, in the face of Governor Andrew's displeasure: "When any community in the United States who have met me in honourable warfare, or even in the prosecution of a rebellious war in an honourable manner, shall call upon me for protection against the nameless horrours of a servile insurrection, they shall have it."

The reader may well ask with surprise if these humane and refined sentiments—and especially the protest against the "legend of infamy" in arming the Negro—were uttered by the same man who now demands the most extravagant rewards for the Negro for his assistance in the war and has tendered the reminiscences of his own beastly and ferocious cruelty to the South as his only title-papers to fame. Unhappily our political history abounds in these enormous self-contradictions of our public men; they have ceased to attract attention; although the intelligent must regard as the worst sign of the moral depravity of a people that condition of public sentiment, in which the inconsistencies of leading men are not only tolerated but actually and positively rewarded. The conversion of such men as Butler to the worst and cruellest purposes of the war is otherwise interesting than in a personal sense; it shows the force and direction of the public sentiment on which such creatures instinctively fastened to save their popularity and on which they rode easily to fame and fortune. The protest we have quoted from Butler might have been a boundary of public opinion in the North, at the time it was written, in the exact and emphatic language we have quoted;

but that opinion soon marched across it and developed a ferocity which the Massachusetts adventurer found it convenient to adopt, and in the increase of which he has acquired all the popularity he possesses to-day. The Negro was first armed; then forcibly emancipated; then used as a partisan instrument; then made a political master, where he had formerly been slave, soldier, freedman; then and now held up as a standing threat, not only of insurrection in the South, but of a war of races, the most terrible exhibition that could possibly be made in the living age. These ascents in cruelty were watched in the progress of the war by the people of the South with increasing anxiety; but they supposed that the summit had been attained at the close of hostilities, and that the list of penalties for the past was complete.

What especially sustained the South in her grief and agony at the end of the war was the instant, lively hope of the restoration of the Union, and the comfort of a speedy re-organization in it. It is remarkable that to the last moment of the war, no one sanely doubted that a reconstruction of the Union would be immediately consequent upon it, while many people in the South had peculiar hopes not only of a speedy, but a generous restoration of rights. Recovery of the Union was the logical conclusion of the contest; it was the professed immediate object of the arms of the government; Congress had proclaimed it, as early as July, 1861—on the eve of the battle of Manassas; and Mr. Lincoln had declared, almost up to the time of the surrender of the Confederate armies, that the war was for the sole purpose of "restoring the Union." It is curious that the only anxiety of Abraham Lincoln was that this restoration might not be expeditious enough after the war, and that it might be necessary to amend the Constitution so as to *compel* the Southern States to send their Senators and Representatives to the Congress at Washington. It is a historical recollection that should be carefully preserved; it is found in a conversation which President Lincoln had with Andrew Johnson, when the latter came to Washington to be inaugurated as Vice-President.* It shows the urgent desire of the former—the "lamented Lincoln"—for a speedy restoration of the Union, even to the point of compulsion of the South to participate again in the common government of the country. Expedition in this matter was shown at his prominent desire, when after the Federal occupation of Richmond, he rode in an open barouche through the streets of that city, scattering smiles and compliments, giving audience and assurance to Richmond editors, pronouncing peace and good-will everywhere, and even on the point of convoking the Virginia Legislature to dispatch the ceremony of restoration.

Surely no one then anticipated the "*problem*" of Reconstruction—that the very object and end of the war was to be constructed into a devious, intricate problem to serve the purposes of a political party, and to defer the hopes of all true patriots. The spectacle and situation to-day is: the constitutional re-union of the States delayed by a political controversy which threatens to last longer than the war itself, *and is quite as dangerous*! There must be some explanation of a condition so unnatural and illogical; this cheat of the intellect and

* The conversation referred to is reported in a speech of President Johnson made on the 22d February, 1866. He testifies that Mr. Lincoln said, speaking of the Southern States: "My great and sole desire has been to preserve these States intact under the Constitution, as they were before; and there should be an amendment to the Constitution which would *compel* the States to send their Senators and Representatives to the Congress of the United States."

common sense of the country that considered the war ended three years ago; this huge intricate afterthought of Reconstruction, on which the South is daily tortured and the whole country hung in suspense.

It is plainly, essentially the afterthought of party; the destructive device of "confusion worse confounded," in which a sinister faction may hide and accomplish their ends; an artificial necessity created for revolutionary and deadly designs. It is thus intelligent men of the South esteem the problem of Reconstruction. They remember how slowly it was invented by Congress; how many delays and changes took place from December, 1865, when the South first presented the issue by sending representatives to Congress, until the Radical plan was finally evolved in its present shape of subjecting the South to the probation of military rule, and the cardinal condition of Negro supremacy; how in this long interval of time there were changes of programme and shiftings of policy and altered devices to the present date of the latest scheme of Reconstruction and its accessories. These, of themselves, are marks of party industry and machinery: not evidences of a straightforward disposition to deal with a plain and obvious necessity. The history of Reconstruction in Congress has been that of the halting and hesitating plot of faction; surely not that of a plain consultation of remedies for a simple, avowed evil.

But for this history we must ask the separate and close attention of the reader before we relate further the condition and temper of the South.

HISTORY OF RECONSTRUCTION.

Need of a popular history of Reconstruction—Declaration of the objects of the war in 1861—Practice of the war as to "existing State institutions"—Cases of Tennessee and Louisiana—Three conditions of restoration—President Lincoln on the "white basis"—Extraordinary proposition of Congress to disfranchise the Negro—Reconstruction policy of President Johnson—Happy condition of the country under it—Gen. Grant's testimony—Necessity of the Republican party— Its revolutionary sentiment and education—Six months of fruitless debate in Congress—Violent premise of Reconstruction—Dogma of forfeited rights—Constitutional Amendment, No 14—Hidden designs of this measure—Trap of Thaddeus Stevens on universal suffrage—A trick on Southern opinion—President Johnson's re-assurances to the South—Reconstruction law of March 2nd, 1867—President's veto—Gen. Grant's interpretation of Reconstruction—History of the Convention elections in the South—Remarkable frauds in the registration—The attempt of Congress upon the President, as part of the Reconstruction scheme—Analysis of this attempt—Three violent measures—A historical remark on the Tenure-of-office law—The significance of impeachment of the President—Its logical identity with Reconstruction.

We propose to write a plain and popular history of Reconstruction. The subject needs such a treatment. It has been so complicated by the multitude of legislative measures, so confused by debate that the public has, in fact, lost all clear and consistent information of it. Scarcely one in a hundred men, even among zealous partisans and those who talk busily of Reconstruction can give an orderly and consecutive narrative of the measures comprised in the topic. We shall endeavour here to give such a narrative, and to disentangle the difficult web of party ingenuity and passion.

The narrative logically and justly commences with the resolution of Congress to which we have referred as adopted in the first year of the war. In this resolution, passed on the 19th July, 1861, it was proclaimed to the world, and immediately noticed to the South—

"That this war is not waged for any purpose of conquest or subjugation, or purpose of overthrowing the Constitutions of those States, but to defend and maintain the supremacy of the Constitution, with all the rights of the several States unimpaired; and *that as soon as these objects are accomplished the war ought to cease.*"

The history of this resolution is remarkable for the deliberation with which it was accomplished, and the peculiar emphasis it obtained from circumstances. It was the first sober thought of the war, the first deliberate judgment that emerged from the confusion and extravagance of passions in which hostilities had commenced. It was also remarkable for its unanimity. The resolution was adopted unanimously by the Senate, and there were only two dissenting voices in the House. It was accepted by the country as expressing honestly and truly the object of the war. It was fortified by the practices of the government, and supplemented by other declarations in the Executive department. The announcement of the war, as to foreign nations, made through Mr. Seward's dispatches, disclaimed the intention of interfering with "existing State institutions," carefully divested it of a single revolutionary design and industriously represented it as a limited and incidental affair of arms that would in no way change the structure of the government. As the war progressed, the practice of the Government was that as its armies advanced over the country that country immediately reverted to its old condition, and was entitled to civil government, and to be represented in Congress. Even when it captured Alexandria, and the flag of the insurgents was actually within sight of the Capitol at Washington, Congress received senators and representatives from the State of Virginia, elected by the people within the Federal lines. As the armies of the Government passed further over the South, there was continued recognition of the legal existence of the States; district attorneys and marshals were appointed; revenue officers collected the tax, and it is remarkable that the Internal Revenue laws describe as States what Congress for other purposes insists now as regarding as waste and conquered territory—willing to recognize these States for financial needs but not for political rights, although the two are inseparable, and their union was consecrated by the blood of 1776.

The first essay of Reconstruction, the first opportunity to test and apply the truth of the declaration referred to, dates from the appointment of Andrew Johnson as Military Governor of Tennessee. The situation then was that the Government had generally resolved to except Slavery from the "institutions" of the Southern States, but in no other respect to impair or diminish the resolution of July 1861. The conditions which then attached to restoration to the Union were only those which implied the extinction of the war and of the measures peculiar to it; this was the boundary, and beyond it no design of interference was ever breathed to suspicion. The *status quo* was to be disturbed only to the extent of abolishing slavery and terminating the war in the sense of abandoning its political measures as well as its arms. Thus the conditions of restoration were distinctly named: that the State should abolish slavery, should repeal the ordinance of secession, and should repudiate the rebel debt. Congress never interfered with this re-organization or reconstruction of the State of Tennessee. The policy was sustained by the Convention which renominated Mr. Lincoln, and by the party which re-elected him in 1864. The definition of the policy was very distinct: it entertained no design upon the local affairs of the State, it did not assume to fix the qualifications of voters or to form Constitutions, it had no other care than that those, who voted and took part in restoring the machinery of government under their Constitutions, had fully, and to the extent of all logical incidents, renounced their rebellion.

The same policy was practically repeated in the case of Louisiana; but it is remarkable that at the time of Mr. Lincoln's death it was suspended by a particular question that had arisen between the President and Congress.

The head of controversy was first raised in the case of Louisiana; it was the first assumption of Congress to take the question of Reconstruction out of the hands of the President. But it was an assumption of the most limited nature and of the most curious effect. It is remarkable that whatever points of difference there were between the President and Congress in the case of Louisiana, there was then no question as to the policy of Reconstruction on the white basis; and that so far from such being the case, Congress expressly excluded the Negro from the right of suffrage in voting for the men who were to frame the new constitutions necessary for admission into the Union. Mr. Lincoln refused to sign the bill to this effect, for other reasons than the exclusion of Negro suffrage; on this point his policy was coincident with that of Congress; and had not the latter been checked as it were by accidental circumstances, it would have committed itself, even beyond the President, to the policy of Reconstruction on the white basis and have shut the door to all its later schemes of Negrophilism.

There was no solicitude for the Negro, beyond what had already been accomplished by Congress in setting him free. "If," confesses a leading Republican—Governor Morton of Indiana— "Mr. Lincoln had not refused to sign that bill, there would be to-day an act of Congress on the statute-books absolutely prohibiting Negroes from participating in the work of re-organization, and pledging the Government in advance to accept of the constitutions that might be formed under the bill, although they made no provision for the Negro beyond the fact of his personal liberty."

Had Mr. Lincoln lived, there is no doubt he would have easily triumphed in his policy of Reconstruction and readily defeated the small faction which Mr. Sumner excited against him in 1865. He had already routed whatever there was of opposition in the Cleveland Convention that had so pretentiously called upon the people "in thunder tones to come to the rescue of impartial justice and universal freedom." He had already triumphed over the protest of Wade and Davis. He was master of the situation, and had he been left to command it, there is every reason to believe that the faction which disturbed him a few days before his death would have been crushed as a paltry annoyance to his popularity—a faction which profiting by accident and the accretion of circumstances and the growth of passions has since assumed the dimensions and the insolence of a dominant party.

President Johnson directly inherited the policy of Mr. Lincoln, and faithfully carried it out until December 1865. He appointed Provisional Governors in the Southern States, and held out inducements to the people to re-organize their governments, and to restore as rapidly as possible their rightful relations to the Union. He even made an addition to Mr. Lincoln's policy in the way of assuring the termination of the war. Recognizing the cardinal idea of this policy to the effect that the people should most fully renounce the ideas of the rebellion and perfect the assurance, that when the Federal armies were withdrawn, the governments left behind should not raise a new rebellion, he prescribed an oath of allegiance and excepted certain persons who had been leading "rebels" from taking part in the re-organization. It was the limit of all real solicitude on the subject; it was a constitutional discretion of the President, both as the organ of clemency in granting pardon and as the head of the army in judging and deciding when it was proper to withdraw and disband it. This new measure of abundant caution was added to the three conditions of restoration: the abolition of slavery, the repeal of the secession ordinance, and the repudiation of the rebel debt; and it was accepted as a logical part of the scheme of Reconstruction.

Under this plain scheme as proposed by President Johnson the country was rapidly quieted; public confidence and prosperity grew visibly under it; and a new animation was imparted to the people of the South. The Provisional Governors proceeded with the re-organization of the State governments by calling Conventions to revise the State Constitutions; and the inducement was held out to the people that a re-organization on this plan would result in a speedy resumption of their electoral privileges, for the choice of State and local officers, and for the election of representatives to Congress from all the States. All the conditions of restoration were performed with singular alacrity and spirit. State after State passed the required ordinances; and when on the 2nd of December, 1865, the legislature of Alabama ratified the Anti-Slavery amendment, Secretary Seward announced with the animation of a great public joy that the vote of this State, "being the twenty-seventh, fills up the complement of two-thirds, and gives the amendment finishing effect as a part of the organic law of the land." The congratulations of the President were conveyed by telegraph. There were indications of the happiest feeling; and it appeared at one time as if all injurious and hateful recollections of the war were about to disappear, and a restoration of peace, the most admirable in history, was to give to the world a crowning manifestation of the greatness and generosity of the American people.

The South had already commenced the realization of an enduring peace; industry was renewed in it, capital sought new fields and enterprises in it, and it was remarkable how all political questions had given way to the renewal and ordinary conversations of commerce. It was a comparatively happy time for the country. In addresses to delegations from the South and in interviews with public men from all parts of the country, President Johnson had frequent occasion in the summer and autumn of 1865 to testify the success of the policy he had inherited from the last part of Mr. Lincoln's administration, and to impart his confidence to the public that it would result in an easy, speedy, and complete restoration of the Union. This confidence was strengthened by Gen. Grant. He made a tour of inspection thro' the South, and the results were officially communicated to the effect, that he was "satisfied that the mass of thinking men of the South accept the present situation of affairs in good faith," and that his observations led him "to the conclusion that the citizens of the Southern States are anxious to return to self-government within the Union as soon as possible." Under this assurance prosperity in all parts of the country improved. The President could not be suspected of partiality for a people whom he had been foremost to punish to the full extent of the war, or of peculiar affection for a policy in which he could not claim the merit of originality. Gen. Grant could not be accused of dullness or of prejudice, since he was then the popular idol; and beyond the cheap sneer of Senator Sumner that his report was a "whitewashing" one, it obtained the unlimited credit of the people, and crowned the vindication of the President's policy.

In this advanced and prosperous condition of public affairs, the Thirty-ninth Congress met in December, 1865. The representatives elect from the Southern States were waiting with their credentials at its doors. It is to be presumed that at this time there occurred to the Republican party in Congress the evident diminution of their political capital, and the obvious prospect of their dissolution as a party, unless they could plant some new controversy on the way of the admission of these Southern representatives and the easy restoration of the Union that would be thereby effected. The wounds of the war had been rapidly healed, and were about being closed. Its animosities had greatly given way to the return of public peace. An easy bridge had by President Johnson's policy been thrown over the chaotic interval that had ensued upon the close of the war. Those who looked on the surface of affairs considered that the Republican party had exhausted its demands; it had freed the Negro, it had punished the "rebel," and it had obtained a guaranty for the continuance of the Union by the most solemn pledges by which they could bind the conscience of the people.

But this view, just and obvious enough, in considering the necessities of the country, misconceived the design of the Republicans, and did not calculate that strong instinct which resides in every political party to perpetuate itself, and to expand its area of controversy. He who writes profoundly and philosophically of these critical times in American history will perceive beneath the surface of events the continuation of that political revolution which had been carried on under cover of the war, and examining closely the further action of the Republican party will detect by a thoughtful diagnosis that what is apparently an unnatural fever is the steady impulses of a logical necessity. The thought repeatedly occurs to the common mind: what was the necessity of this continued revolutionary movement against the Constitution, since the Republican party had accomplished the abolition of Slavery?—is the Constitution naturally vicious?—has it not, apart from the subject of Slavery, otherwise proved a beneficent system of government? The answer is that the necessity of this revolutionary movement is the necessity of a party. When we thoughtfully contemplate the political history of our country we find that the Anti-Slavery party was necessarily the party of Consolidation; to accomplish the abolition of Slavery, it was forced to accept the theory of a consolidated government; but the special object accomplished, the idea survives, the force of a revolutionary education continues, and a party impelled by such influences and by the necessity, supreme to it, of continuing its organization, is not long in finding new measures with which to engage public attention.

It was in this thoughtful attitude, meditating this necessity, that the Republican party stood in December, 1865. It had no idea of approving the President's policy; but the difficult question was to invent measures of opposition, sufficiently plausible, to a plan of action that had progressed far in public favour, and had already borne the most grateful fruits. The work was commenced at once; but we shall see how long and laboured it was. The Southern representatives were rejected, even at roll-call, when the House was organized. A "Joint Committee on Reconstruction" was raised, "to inquire into the condition" of the Southern States, and various calls for information were made upon the Executive departments.

For six long, fruitless months this Committee sat, before it relieved public curiosity or favoured Congress with a formal report. Its sessions were secret; but we must suppose that its invention was severely taxed, and its counsels greatly confused, by the number of raw and unsatisfactory measures which, from time to time, emanated from it before its final report was made. These measures were imperfect and conflicting; they were scarcely more than sops to the curiosity which clamoured at the door of the "star chamber" for information of its proceedings. First, Mr. Stevens reported from it an amendment to the Constitution, to the effect of excluding from the basis of representation all who were denied the elective franchise "on account of race or colour." The proposition was worried with amendments and substitutes, and at last went back to the Committee without instructions. Mr. Bingham came forward next, with another Constitutional amendment, proposing to give Congress the power to make certain laws for the government of all the States. It was recommitted, reported again, postponed in the House and never again called up; "laid over" in the Senate and not again considered. A remarkable hesitation was evident in Congress; a hesitation which scarcely belongs to the consultation of any plain public necessity and which is irresistibly suggestive of the embarrassed counsels of party expediency.

At last, on the 18th June, 1866, came the long-expected birth; and on that day there was submitted in both Houses of Congress the formal report of the Joint Committee on Reconstruction. It is not necessary, here, to review this formidable document and its long trains of argument; and it suffices for our narrative to place here its conclusion. It was startling enough: that the Southern States had "*forfeited all civil and political rights and privileges under the Constitution!*" It is to be remarked that the report of the Committee recommended no distinct policy, that it proposed no definite means, immediate or prospective, for the re-admission to representation of the Southern States; but its importance was, that in the broad proposition with which it concluded—and which was accepted by a party vote in each branch of Congress—it furnished sufficient basis for almost any extent of revolutionary action with regard to the States so summarily and entirely condemned.

Congress had now put under its feet the ground of a dogma, but it yet hesitated as to the policy and form of measure it would construct upon it. A feeble minority had made no issue as to the power of Congress to take the subject of "Reconstruction" out of the hands of the President; there was no question of jurisdiction; and Mr. Reverdy Johnson who made the minority report in the House from the Joint Committee had "not thought it necessary to examine into the legality of the measures adopted, either by the late or present President," and had been satisfied to relieve their motives from censure in declaring that "the sole object of each was to effect a complete and early union of all the States." The situation now was, that Congress had not only reclaimed control, complete and exclusive, of the subject of "Reconstruction," but had also, by accepting the report of its Committee, thrown off the restraints of the Constitution, with respect to ten States, and had taken a *carte blanche* for legislation!

The first distinct measure offered on this settlement of principles, and which, in point of time, preceded the formal report on "Reconstruction" was Constitutional Amendment, No. 14. We give it in the words, in which, after an extraordinary perplexity of verbal amendments, it finally passed Congress on the 13th June, 1866;

ARTICLE XIV

SECTION 1. All persons born or naturalized in the United States, and subject to the jurisdiction thereof, are citizens of the United States, and of the State wherein they reside. No State shall make or enforce any law which shall abridge the privileges or immunities of citizens of the United States; nor shall any State deprive any person of life, liberty, or property without due process of law, nor deny to any person within its jurisdiction the equal protection of the laws.

SEC. 2. Representatives shall be apportioned among the several States according to their respective numbers, counting the whole number of persons in each State, excluding Indians not taxed. But when the right to vote at any election for the choice of electors for President and Vice-President of the United States, representatives in Congress, the executive and judicial officers of a State, or the members of the Legislature thereof, is denied to any of the male inhabitants of such State, being twenty-one years of age and citizens of the United States, or in any way abridged, except for participation in rebellion or other crime, the basis of representation therein shall be reduced in the proportion which the number of such male citizens shall bear to the whole number of male citizens, twenty-one years of age, in such State.

SEC. 3. No person shall be a senator or representative in Congress, or elector of President or Vice-President, or hold any office, civil or military, under the United States or under any State, who, having previously taken an oath as a member of Congress, or as an officer of the United States, or as a member of any State Legislature, or as an executive or judicial officer of any State, to support the Constitution of the United States, shall have engaged in insurrection or rebellion against the same, or giving aid or comfort to the enemies thereof. But Congress may, by a vote of two-thirds of each House, remove such disability.

SEC. 4. The validity of the public debt of the United States authorized by law, including debts incurred for payment of pensions and bounties for services in suppressing insurrection or rebellion, shall not be questioned. But neither the United States nor any State shall assume to pay any debt or obligation incurred in aid of insurrection or rebellion against the United States, or any claim for the loss or emancipation of any slave; but all such debts, obligations, and claims shall be held illegal and void.

SEC. 5. The Congress shall have power to enforce, by appropriate legislation, the provisions of this article.

We shall presently see what designs lurked in this plausible law. Indeed, Mr. Thaddeus Stevens has recently exposed the fact that the first clause was designed to entrap Congress on the subject of Negro suffrage; claiming that the declaration of the citizenship of the Negro carried with it the right of suffrage as among those "privileges and immunities" which the State was prohibited from abridging. Whatever may be the merit of this claim (and we shall elsewhere recur to it in a legal argument with which we cannot now conveniently attend our narrative), it is certain that it was studiously concealed in recommending and perfecting the passage of the bill. It was well known to the country that the original Constitution of the United States did not define citizenship; questions in this respect had been raised on it; and the object of the Amendment No. 14, was apparently, in its first clause, to supply an omission in the original instrument, to terminate a controversy, and to determine a rule of citizenship in opposition to the decision of the Supreme Court in the Dred Scott case, that the descendant of an African, born within the United States, was not a citizen. It was never suspected at the time that the words of the Amendment had the meaning or intention which Mr. Stevens now ascribes to them; that they were designed thus readily to capture the sense of the country on a subject, which, so far from being an easy and foregone conclusion, we find in every form of public expression outside the Amendment, occupied by the most eager and passionate controversy.

But there was another trick, another legislative device in this Amendment more remarkable. It went for ratification to all the States as an undivided proposition. But there is certain evidence that the Republican party in Congress, while making an effort at sincerity, had secretly determined to effect and to insure its rejection by the Southern States, with the view of using such rejection for its own political purposes, and making it the occasion and excuse for additional measures of severity towards the people of the South. Such a rejection could not have been better been insured than by the violent and *impossible* condition inserted in the third section, calling upon the people of the South to disfranchise and to dishonour all the men in whom they had ever placed any public confidence—all who had ever held any office, State or Federal. It was really no test of the loyal sentiment of the South; for men, however loyal to the Union, however converted to a political principle, could not but see the staring injustice, the cowardly cruelty of betraying those men especially whom they had trusted in the past, and of condemning them for simply doing what they themselves had done. In this light the proposition was viewed in the South with an unanimity, from which was excluded all debate as to mere political concerns. It was a sentimentalism above all questions of politics. The people were asked to strike the bosoms of their friends with a serpent's tooth; to give up all the tender and reverential memories of their dead; to put badges of dishonour on the maimed bodies of their heroes, men who, no matter that it was in a lost and mistaken cause, had bled and suffered and toiled for the mass of their countrymen; to make a vicarious sacrifice of their best and bravest; to pay the price of cowardly safety in the guilt of most unnatural treachery! The Republican party in Congress had safely calculated that the people of the South were infinitely above such a concession of their affections. The very impossibility of the condition is proof that there was no sincere design in offering it, that its acceptance was neither expected nor desired, that it was part of a suspicious diplomacy.

There is other proof of this. On the 8th June, in the Senate, Mr. Doolittle made a motion to allow the several provisions of the Amendment to be separately submitted and voted upon. He explained that the 3d section would inevitably defeat the ratification in every Southern State; the division he proposed was a fair one in a case where, indeed, there was no logical connexion, and where the purpose should have been to obtain as distinctly as possible the sense of the South, even at some expense of legislative convenience. The motion was defeated; an unyielding majority adhered to what had been plotted in caucus; and the obnoxious section was left to drag down the whole measure, and to entrap the South into what were to be violently taken as declarations of disloyalty.

As thus foreseen, the Amendment was rejected by the Southern States; besides the ten included in the rebellion, Kentucky, Delaware and Maryland voting against it. Tennessee was the only geographically Southern State that voted for it. From the other States, the two thirds vote necessary to ratify it was obtained, and having become a part of the Constitution it appeared to have passed from public attention. Indeed, after Tennessee was admitted into the Union (July 24, 1866,) the press appears to have given but little attention to the further course of the Amendment, beyond a stray and naked telegram, now and then, announcing the vote of each State.

Meanwhile President Johnson, although obstructed in the work he had assumed in reorganizing the Southern States, continued in other directions, wherever his jurisdiction applied, his policy of conciliation and generosity. He re-assured the people of the South by various proclamations. On the 30th August, 1866, he issued a proclamation declaring the state of war ended, and civil authority existing throughout the United States. A few weeks later, he issued an amnesty proclamation, modifying the proclamation of May 29, 1865, wherein "fourteen extensive classes of persons were altogether excepted and excluded from the benefits thereof," so that "the full and beneficent pardon conceded" in that proclamation "should be opened and further extended to a large number of the persons who, by its aforesaid exceptions, have been hitherto excluded from Executive clemency."

The second session of the Thirty-ninth Congress commenced on the 3d December, 1866. The rejection by the Southern States of "Constitutional Amendment", No. 14, had supplied the step to a new scheme of "Reconstruction" to which might be added a measure of revenge; and on the second day of the session the Committee on Territories was set to work, on the basis of a resolution describing the South as "several districts of country" formerly occupied by "the once existing States." Several schemes were proposed; but the general idea appears to have been maintained that the Amendment or its equivalent should be forced upon the Southern States; and the final result was to put it in the aggravated form of the following general law of Reconstruction, coupling it with the preliminary conditions of military rule, and the immediate concession of Negro suffrage,—the most unconstitutional and violent compulsions of the popular will that could be well imagined.

An Act to provide efficient government for the insurrectionary States.

Whereas, No legal State government or adequate protection for life or property now exist in the Rebel States of Virginia, North Carolina, South Carolina, Georgia, Alabama, Mississippi, Louisiana, Florida, Texas, and Arkansas; *and whereas*, it is necessary that peace and good order should be enforced in said States until loyal and republican State governments can be legally established; therefore

Be it enacted, etc., That said Rebel States shall be divided into military districts and made subject to the military authority of the United States, as hereinafter mentioned; and for that purpose Virginia shall constitute the First District, North Carolina and South Carolina the Second District, Georgia, Alabama, and Florida the Third District, Mississippi and Arkansas the Fourth District, and Louisiana and Texas the Fifth District.

SEC. 2. That it shall be the duty of the President to assign to the command of each of said districts an officer of the army not below the rank of Brigadier-General, and to detail a sufficient military force to enable such officer to perform his duties and enforce his authority within the district to which he is assigned.

SEC. 3. That it shall be the duty of each officer assigned as aforesaid to protect all persons in their rights of person and property, to suppress insurrection, disorder, and violence, and to punish or cause to be punished all disturbers of the public peace and criminals; and to this end he may allow local civil tribunals to take jurisdiction of and try offenders, or, when in his judgment it may be necessary for the trial of offenders, he shall have power to organize military committees or tribunals for that purpose; and all interference under colour of State authority with the exercise of military authority under this act shall be null and void.

SEC. 4. That all persons put under military arrest by virtue of this act shall be tried without unnecessary delay, and no cruel or unusual punishment shall be inflicted, and no sentence of any military com mission or tribunal hereby authorized, affecting the life or liberty of any person, shall be executed until it is approved by the officer in command of the district; and the laws and regulations for the government of the army shall not be effected by this act, except in so far as they may conflict with its provisions. *Provided,* That no sentence of death under this act shall be carried into execution without the approval of the President.

SEC. 5. When the people of any one of said Rebel States shall have formed a constitution and government in conformity with the Constitution of the United States in all respects, framed by a convention of delegates elected by the male citizens of said State, 21 years old and upward, of whatever race, colour, or previous condition, who have been resident in said State for one year previous to the day of election, except such as may be disfranchised for participation in the Rebellion or for felony at common law, and when such constitution shall provide that the elective franchise shall be enjoyed by all such persons as have the qualifications herein stated for electors of delegates, and when such constitution shall be ratified by a majority of the persons voting on the question of ratification who are qualified as electors for delegates, and when such constitution shall have been submitted to Congress for examination and approval, and Congress shall have approved the same, and when said State by a vote of its Legislature elected under said constitution shall have adopted the amendment to the Constitution of the United States proposed by the XXXIXth Congress, and known as Article 14, and when said article shall have become part of the Constitution of the United States, said State shall be declared entitled to representation in Congress, and Senators and Representatives shall be admitted therefrom on their taking the oath prescribed by law, and then and thereafter the preceding sections of this act shall be inoperative in said State. *Provided,* That no person excluded from the privilege of holding office by said proposed amendment to the Constitution of the United States shall be eligible to election as a member of the convention to frame a constitution for any of said Rebel States, nor shall any such person vote for members of such convention.

SEC. 6. Until the people of the said Rebel States shall by law be admitted to representation in the Congress of the United States, all civil governments that may exist therein shall be deemed provisional only, and shall be in all respects subject to the paramount authority of the United States, at any time to abolish, modify, control, and supersede the same, and in all elections to any office under such provisional governments all persons shall be entitled to vote under the provisions of the fifth section of this act. And no person shall be eligible to any office under such provisional governments who would be disqualified from holding office under the provisions of the third article of said Constitutional Amendment.

This extraördinary law was passed on the 2nd March, 1867. A second or Supplemental act, relating mainly to the registration of voters, referred to in the 5th section, was passed March 23d, 1867, at the first session of the Fortieth Congress; and a third or Explanatory act was passed July 19th, 1867, at an extra session, in effect declaring that the military government over the ten States was to have unlimited authority over the Courts, and over all the offices of the State, legislative, executive and judicial.

There was thus absolutely erected in ten States a mode of vice-royal rule outside of the Constitution. In a veto message of surpassing intellectual power the President pointed out the despotism, the political purpose and the unconstitutionality of the law of the 2nd March. He summed his objections in this remarkable sentence: "I submit to Congress whether this measure is not, in its whole character, scope and object, without precedent and without authority, in palpable conflict with the plainest provisions of the Constitution, and utterly destructive to those great principles of liberty and humanity for which our ancestors on both sides of the Atlantic have shed so much blood and expended so much treasure."

The history of the execution of this law is as yet incomplete. We may say, however, generally that it has afforded an example of *unlimited* power, such as the modern world has seldom known. "The law," says Gen. Grant, "makes the district commanders *their own interpreters* of their power or duty under it; and, in my opinion, the Attorney General or myself can do no more than give our opinion of the meaning of the law." Each commander has placed his own construction upon the acts of Congress; and we may imagine how illimitable is the assumption of authority, how petty and invasive is the tyranny when we find it carried to the length of an order forbidding the police of a city to wear gray uniform, and another forbidding the distillation of grain.

But the most remarkable thing in the history of this viceroyal rule in the South is the manipulation of elections; the frauds in registration; the injustice of the apportionment, which, with a large white majority in all the States, so arranged the districts, as to insure a majority to the Negroes in the Conventions called to frame the organic law. The general nature of our narrative admits no more than a summary view of the outrage. It is well known that there is a large preponderance of white population in all of the excluded States; yet the registration process produced the result of the political ascendancy of the Negro throughout most of them. In Florida, where the whites by the last census were 77,747 to 62,637, the registering officers allowed 4,733 whites and 9,388 blacks to vote. In Georgia, notwithstanding forty thousand whites of that State had been disfranchised, it still had a registered majority of about two thousand whites; yet the districts were so laid out as to allow 93,417 blacks to elect 192 delegates and 95,303 whites to elect 65 delegates to the State Convention. In Alabama, the majority of the blacks in the registration was 15,561, and the number of blacks enrolled showed an increase of over 90,000 since 1860. In Texas there was a black majority of 10,000, though the census of

1860 showed 420,891 whites to 183,021 blacks. In Louisiana, where Gen. Banks at the close of the war reported the blacks had fallen off one-fourth, the registers footed up 82, 907 blacks, which taking the usual ratio of population to voters in that State exhibits an increase of 193,000 blacks in seven years, or fully fifty-five per cent. In Virginia, where the whites had 13,000 registered majority, the apportionment of districts was so made that in 46 districts the whites had a majority and in 59 the blacks had a majority, giving a black majority in Convention of thirteen. These facts are important as a remarkable array of evidence of a steady and unscrupulous design to Africanize the South, and after torturing it with military law to pass it to the control of the Negro. Military rule and Negro supremacy become the short definition of "Reconstruction."*

* We may place here the proceedings of the Supreme Court properly episodical to Reconstruction.

1. A petition on behalf of the States of Georgia and Mississippi for an injunction to restrain the President and district commanders from carrying out the provisions of the Reconstruction laws. Adverse decision April 15th, 1867; Chief Justice Chase delivering the opinion of the court, maintaining the impropriety of interference, and, generally, that an injunction against the execution of an act of Congress by the incumbent of the Presidential office cannot be received, whether it describes him as President, or simply as a citizen of a State. Motion for leave to file a bill, therefore, dismissed.

2. A bill in which the State of Georgia is complainant against Edwin M. Stanton, Ulysses S. Grant, and John Pope. Leave was granted to file the bill *nem. con.*, and subpœnas have been issued.

3. "The McCardle case." Appeal from the Circuit Court of Mississippi dismissing *habeas corpus* and remanding the prisoner to the military authority. He had been originally arrested by a military order and tried by a military commission on specifications of having obstructed the Reconstruction laws and slandered a military officer of the United States, etc. in certain criticisms in a newspaper which the prisoner published in the town of Vicksburg. The case was brought before the Circuit Court on a writ of *habeas corpus*; but the court decided it had no jurisdiction, and the prisoner was remanded. On these facts the case came before the Supreme Court, was elaborately argued, but was finally ordered over to the next term. Whereupon the following protest was signed by Judge Grier, a member of the Court:—"The case was fully argued in the beginning of this month" (March, 1868). "It is a case which not only involves the liberty and rights of the appellant, but of millions of our fellow-citizens. The country had a right to expect, it would receive the immediate and solemn attention of the court By the postponement of this case, this court has subjected itself, whether justly or un-

But we are occupied in this place only with a narrative of the events which fill in the scheme of Reconstruction; and to complete this narrative, we must pass to a new series of measures. We refer to that train of acts of Congress by which it has sought to fetter the President of the United States, to annul all possible efforts at interference or obstruction by the Executive authority with respect to ten States of the Union, and to impair so far the constitutional functions of his office. This attempt upon the President is a necessary part of the Congressional scheme of Reconstruction; it has moved at equal pace with it; and running with the measures already referred to, has been a series of outrages and usurpations upon his authority. They are summarily stated as follows—

1. A bill, which became a law in January, 1867, repealing the 13th section of the Act of July 17th, 1862, authorizing the President by proclamation "to extend to persons who may have participated in the existing rebellion * * pardon and amnesty."

justly, to the imputation that it had evaded the performance of a duty imposed upon it by the Constitution, and awaited for legal interposition to supersede its action, and relieve it of responsibility. I have only to say, *Pudet hoc opprobrio, licet non potuisse repelli*, or literally translated, 'I am ashamed such an opprobrium should be cast upon the court, and that it cannot be refuted.' "

The common explanation of the postponement is that the Supreme Court was generally supposed to have reached a decision in the McCardle case, prior to the Impeachment proceedings, and from the known inclination of a majority of the court it was believed that the decision, when promulgated, would be adverse to the constitutionality of the military governments in the South. The Radicals contemplated the possibility of such a result, and regarded it with great alarm. They viewed it with exclusive reference to its effect upon the coming Presidential election, and very justly with great apprehension. It would have been simply a condemnation of the policy of Congress—a declaration from the highest legal authority that the whole system of Radical Reconstruction was illegal and unconstitutional. A resort was, therefore, had to legislation, ignoring the Supreme Court so far as its jurisdiction might affect Radical Reconstruction. The law was passed, vetoed, passed over the veto; and it was this enactment, the constitutionality of which was to have been argued. The McCardle case had been fully argued and submitted for decision, and the delay in the promulgation of its *ultimatum* is what Judge Grier pronounces the evasion of a duty imposed by the Constitution.

2. An Act, March 2, 1867, virtually depriving the President of his constitutional functions as Commander-in-Chief of the Army. It provides that the head-quarters of the General of the army shall be at Washington, and all orders and instructions relating to military operations issued by the President or Secretary of War shall be issued through the General of the army, and, in case of his inability, through the next in rank; that the General of the army shall not be removed, suspended, or relieved from command, or assigned to duty elsewhere than at said head-quarters, except at his own request, without the previous approval of the Senate; and any orders or instructions relating to military operations issued contrary to the requirements of this section shall be null and void; and any officer who shall issue orders or instructions contrary to the provisions of this section shall be deemed guilty of a misdemeanor in office; and any officer of the army who shall transmit, convey, or obey any orders or instructions so issued contrary to the provisions of this section, knowing that such orders were so issued, shall be liable to imprisonment for not less than two nor more than twenty years, upon conviction thereof in any court of competent jurisdiction.

3. What is popularly known as "the Tenure of Office Bill," passed March 2, 1867. By this law the President is forbidden to remove from office those appointed by him, with the advice and consent of the Senate, unless the Senate consent to such removal, and it is made a high misdemeanor for him to appoint others in their places, or for such others to accept said appointment.

It has been remarked especially of this last extraordinary law that the question of the power of removal had been settled, as early as 1789, in the first Congress under the Constitution;

that, when the Department of State was created, a declaratory clause was inserted in the bill of affirmation that this power was vested in the President; and that Congress repeated the decision or legislative construction twice afterwards in creating executive departments. The point was made in the unavailing veto of the President; but we do not design to introduce argument here, and have merely mentioned it as a part of the history of the law of 1867.

In looking at these three measures, the reflection at once occurs to the reader, that besides being a subordinate part of the scheme of Reconstruction, they amount to a revolutionary design upon the cardinal and vital distribution of powers in our system of government. At a later date the attempt upon the President traced in these measures—diminishing the prerogative of pardon, taking from him the control of the army, and impairing his duty to see that the laws are "faithfully executed," by cutting off the power of removal incidental to that duty—has progressed to the extremity of Impeachment. It is an unbroken sequence; Impeachment, so far from a distinct incident, being the logical fruit of the whole tenour and spirit of Reconstruction, that point to which a consistant revolutionary purpose has steadily mounted.

We are aware that an attempt has been made to wrest Impeachment from its proper historical connection, to dissociate it from Reconstruction, and to misrepresent it as an event of no practical consequence, designing a mere change of Presidents, after which the government might resume its routine, and the country take up the thread of its daily cares as before. But we abstain from argument here, reserving it for another place in this work, where we shall have occasion to describe Impeachment as something more than a spectacular drama at Washington. It is sufficient to say of it in this place, that the interest of the revolutionary movement that has taken the name and pretences of Reconstruction has culminated at this point; and we conveniently terminate here what was designed as a task of pure narrative. With patient detail we have given over the history of Reconstruction;—the abundant commentary on it we reserve for other places, and shall put under appropriate heads.

THREE NOTABLE ARGUMENTS.

The three arguments for the Reconstruction scheme of Congress—Senator Sumner's early discovery of "dead States"—A clear and fundamental proposition—Decision of Justice Sprague of Massachusetts—Estoppel of Congress from the doctrine of State forfeiture—Important decision of Chief Justice Chase on the North Carolina Circuit—The argument of a "conquered country"—Extract from an English statesman—"*Occupatio bellica*"—The Constitutional guaranty of a Republican form of government—Senator Sumner's ignorance of history—Analysis of the Constitution with respect to suffrage—The general argument for universal suffrage—Recent declamations of Thaddeus Stevens—A logical reply to them—Universal suffrage, as meaning Negro suffrage for the South—A brutal mockery of republicanism.

The arguments to sustain that new political system, of which we have already given the history, are scattered through debates in Congress, through various proceedings in the Supreme Court, and through daily expressions of a partisan press. We know that the public mind has been strained and confused by this multitude of arguments, and the diversity of the channels through which they have found expression. We think it interesting, therefore, to collect them, to put them in order, and to pass them in review. We propose to do so in a popular way. We shall avoid the prolix methods of the mere lawyer; and we shall take care not to annoy the reader by that puerile style of numerical arguments, the ambition of which is to make of its subject the largest number of divisions and subdivisions. There are plainly not more than three general heads of the argument and when we have reviewed them, we have traversed the whole field of the controversy.

1. We have the argument that the Southern States and their people forfeited their rights by the rebellion.

2. We are entertained by the theory that these States have been reduced by the war to conquered territory, and that Congress may govern them by the right of conquest.

3. We are told that the United States are bound to guarantee a republican form of government to every State in the Union, and are in the exercise of that power with respect to the Southern States in the present scheme of "Reconstruction."

From these three points we may stake out the boundaries of the whole field of discussion, and complete our popular survey of the question. We believe that all that has been said or written on Reconstruction may be placed without violence under the arguments we have noted, and that when we have completed these we have arrived at a fair and sufficient conclusion on the subject.

The first of these arguments is the earliest in the history of the discussion, and, indeed, dates from the commencement of the war. Its first appearance was in a loose passionate language threatening the belligerent rebels, and scarcely attracting attention at the time but as a display of declamatory rhetoric. It was of a piece with those avowals of vengeance growing out of the heat of the war, and too readily supposed to be mere exclamations of passion. When during the war an intemperate Republican declared in Congress that the war should "make a pathway of desolation fron the Potomac to the Gulf of Mexico;" when another was for "crushing" his erring countrymen as "infernal, damnable fiends;" when another recommended that the "rebels" should be treated "as devils—not only their personal goods, and their lives, but the fee simple of their lands be taken from them;" and when yet another said that neither South Carolina, Georgia or Florida "should re-appear in the Union; let these States be set apart as a home for the Negro!"—but few of the public were disposed to accept these expressions in a serious and literal sense, or to esteem them more than the exaggerated utterances of hate. But in this frenzy lurked a "method of madness," and from these wild expressions grew the monstrous idea which the Republican party has since deliberately advanced, to the effect that the Southern States having forfeited their rights in the war are left with no other government than the punitive will of Congress. It is interesting to observe how this splutter of malice has at last arranged itself into the serious form of argument.

We find it first reduced to an orderly proposition by Senator Sumner and announced in a series of resolutions introduced by him in the United States Senate, February, 1862, to this effect: that a vote of secession from the Union, sustained by force, "becomes a practical *abdication* by the State of all rights under the Constitution; while the treason which it involves still further works an instant *forfeiture* of all those functions and powers essential to the continued existence of the State as a body politic, so that from that time forward the territory falls under the exclusive jurisdiction of Congress as other territory, and the State, being, according to the language of the law, *felo-de-se*, ceases to exist." Since this rhetorical accumulation of Mr. Sumner, public attention has been diverted by a number of captious and convenient phrases to indicate this singular decease of the "rebel" States. We have had, indeed, a plentiful supply of catch-words on the subject. Senator Wilson makes a short cut to the doctrine of his colleague in the words "dead States." Further we are told of "State abdication," "State forfeiture," "State suicide," "the lapsing of States into territories," etc. Mr. Thaddeus Stevens, with the unsightly effort of age at a brutal and malicious joke, thus paraphrases Reconstruction: "Congress passed an act authorizing waste Territories of the United States to form Constitutions, if possible, so as to make them fit to be associated with civilized communities."

The one argument on which all these conceits of language are strung is that the Southern people are outlaws, having forfeited their rights, even those of local government, by the act of withdrawing from the United States. The argument is so violent and excessive as to carry its own refutation with it and to destroy itself by the mere force of its declaration. It is in fact saying that because the "rebel" States denied the right of the Federal government to keep them in the Union, that therefore that right did not exist, and that they have really and practically accomplished "Secession" in continuing out of the Union despite the decision of the war and the virtue of the Federal arms. The mere statement of such a case in the form of a question should be decisive of the answer. The supposition of "dead States," "States out of the Union," is essentially and unavoidably either the admission of the legal virtue of Secession, or the claim that Congress has the right to expel States from the Union!

There is one thought which firmly fixed in the mind gives a clear view of the whole subject of Reconstruction and rescues from confusion its entire multitude of issues. It is simply that *the Government has acquired no new political power by the war*, that in respect of its power and constitutional authority it is the same continuous government that it was before the war. In such case says Mr. Justice Sprague of Massachusetts, "the nation acquires no new sovereignty, but merely maintains its previous rights. Under our Government the right of sovereignty over any portion of a State is given and limited by the Constitution, and will be the same after the war as it was before."* The language of this judicial decision has the merit of explicitness, and for this may please the reader; but it is unnecessary as an addition by way of argument to what is not only morally a truism, but is to be found in the very body of the Constitution of the United States. We find that the Constitution prohibits even the nation from depriving any State of its "equal suffrage in the Senate;"† and in view of this provision, how can the assumption be held that Congress may expel States from the Union, or even exercise an extraordinary and despotic rule over them!

Since, then, the Government has acquired no addition of sovereignty, no new political power by the war, and since furthermore its relations to the States and power over the States are limited by the Constitution, we are safely left to the conclusion that it can neither expel nor diminish a State, without violating the organic law or incurring the guilt of usurpation.

It is curious to notice what inconsistencies have been mixed with the absurdities of this doctrine of the death or diminution of the Southern States by forfeiture of their rights on account of their rebellion. In various acts of Congress assuming these States to be still within the Union, it has made a deliberate and accumulated estoppel to the doctrine that they are excluded, or that they have not subsisting valid State governments.

* Case of Amy Warwick, 24 Law Rep. decided at one of the terms of 1862

† Article V.

Even during the war Congress repeatedly legislated for them as States still within the Union, and, in 1862, by the apportionment bill gave each of these States their proper proportion of representatives in the national legislature. At the close of the war it yet more strongly committed itself; and in receiving the ratification of the Constitutional Amendment abolishing Slavery by the legislatures of the Southern States, it recognized them as exercising the very highest legislative functions in our political system and performing an act of supreme importance. Yet this act is invalid on the supposition that the Southern States were not in the Union, for the ratifications of at least three of them had to be counted to carry the amendment; and the consequence is that Slavery has never been constitutionally extinguished and that there is no guaranty that it may not be reclaimed and re-established. To such absurdities are we forced by the doctrine of dead or decayed States, having no right of representation in the Union, and no political existence but as the subject of despotic will.

We have thus rapidly gone over the first and capital ground of the Republican party in the scheme of Reconstruction, with the arguments suggesting themselves to a plain mind. These arguments, however, are assisted from an unexpected quarter. Happily, on the subject we have been considering, there is the light of a distinct judicial decision, the force and importance of which appear to have been but little appreciated in the political controversy, or in the popular discussion. A ruling made by Chief Justice Chase, sitting at Raleigh, North Carolina, in June, 1867, has, after a strange neglect, recently been brought to public attention, and is found to be a clear and irrevocable decision of the inviolability of the Union, and of the present residence of all the States in it in their original character and condition. The essential part of the opinion of the Chief Justice is thus stated:

"There is no doubt that the State of North Carolina, by the acts of the Convention of May, 1861, by the previous acts of the Governor of the State, by subsequent acts of all the departments of the State Government, and by the acts of the people at the election held after May, 1861, set aside her State Government and Constitution, and connected under the National Constitution with the Government of the United States, and established a Constitution, and Government, connected with another pretended Government set up in hostility to the United States, and entered upon a course of active warfare against the National Government; nor is there any doubt that, by these acts, the practical relations of North Carolina to the Union were suspended, and very serious liabilities incurred by those who were engaged in them.

"*But these acts did not effect, even for a moment, the separation of North Carolina from the Union, any more than the acts of an individual who commits grave offences against the State by resisting its officers and defying its authority, can separate him from the State.*"

It thus appears that the ordinances and other acts of secession on the part of the Southern States, in the words of the Chief Justice, merely "suspended" "the practical relations" of these States to the Union. This "suspension," having been caused by these ordinances and acts, ceases when they are annulled by the war, and therefore the prior relations of these States are restored, and they are entitled to all the privileges of the Union and bound by all its obligations. In addition to what is quoted above, the Chief Justice expressly repudiates the doctrine that the "insurgent States, by the act of rebellion, and by levying war against the nation, became foreign States." Then if not foreign States, they must have been States of the Union; nothing has occurred since the war to change their character; therefore they must be such

States now. The whole argument at last is reduced to this simple syllogism and the conclusion is as inviolable as it is plain.

We advance to the second argument of the Republicans. And the moment we confront it, an odious phrase seizes attention and excites our suspicion. The world has outlived those convenient words of tyranny grown out of violent and barbarous times—a "conquered country!" It is remarkable how peculiarly these words have been used to justify oppression, and to disguise the rod of the tyrant in the robe of the conqueror. It is memorable as the precise argument which Great Britain used for the oppression of our fathers; the pretence which the celebrated Blackstone, to the lasting injury of his great legal reputation, furnished to Charles II. for abusing and grinding the American Colonies. America was a "conquered country," and therefore at the merciful disposition of the Crown! The dishonour of this plea has alone survived wherever it has been made. It did not serve to exculpate England in her oppression of the Colonies, or in her later maltreatment of Ireland. We are told by a recent historian that, when arbitrary government was planted in Ireland, there were those in the British Parliament who excused it because the Irish were a conquered nation; whereupon there was this exclamation on the part of a distinguished statesman: "They were 'a conquered nation!'" cries Pym.

"There cannot be a word more pregnant and fruitful in treason than that is. There are few nations in the world that have not been conquered, and no doubt the conqueror may give what law he pleases to those that are conquered; but if the succeeding acts and agreements do not limit and restrain that right, what people can be secure? England hath been conquered, and Wales hath been conquered, and by this reason will be in little better case than Ireland. If the king, by the right of a conqueror, gives laws to his people, shall not the people by the same reason be restored to the right of the conquered, to recover their liberty, if they can?"

The argument of the English statesman is full of sense and humanity. But the disgraced plea which the Congress at Washington applies to its scheme of Reconstruction in the South, even if it could be just in any circumstances, is wholly inappropriate here; there is no case of the conqueror; and it is impossible to force an analogy between one nation overcoming another, and a government merely recovering its own territory and re-asserting its authority over its own subjects. The plea is so absurd and incoherent that it is almost impossible to engage it in serious argument. The idea of conquest by a Government of its own territory borders on the ridiculous. Again we quote from that decision of Judge Sprague, to which we have already referred: "No nation ever makes conquest of its own territory. If a hostile power, either from without or from within, takes and holds possession and dominion over any portion of its territory, and the nation by force of arms expels or overthrows the enemy and suppresses hostilities, it acquires no new title, but merely regains the possession of which it had been temporarily deprived."

Absurd as is the plea which applies the rule of conquest to

a civil war, we are aware there is a legal refinement of it which has obtained a certain attention. The air of subtlety is the natural one of absurdity, and nonsense readily takes refuge in a confusion of ideas. Thus, we are told, that throwing out the consideration of the rule of conquest, the Government has yet the right of hostile "occupation" in the Southern States, and that Congress may therefore take their affairs into its hands. But this argument is really inferiour to that of conquest, as the greater includes the less; for the "*occupatio bellica*" contained in the right of conquest is the lesser right, and they fall together. If after the war the army of the United States remains in the South, it is yet no hostile occupation in a legal sense; and though we freely admit, that it may quell insurrection and keep the peace in its neighbourhood, we utterly deny that even in a case of utter anarchy it could force institutions upon the country. The distinction is obvious between an affair of police and a usurpation of power to the extent of seizing the government of a country and dictating its political institutions. "What right," says a distinguished advocate, speaking at the bar of the Supreme Court, in a recent case of individual oppression under the Reconstruction laws, "has the army of a sovereign occupying his own territory, when every hostile force is subdued, to take in its own hands the government of the country by a right paramount to the antecedent right?"

We come to the third argument: that the guaranty in the Constitution of a republican form of government justifies the claim of Congress and imposes upon it the duty to intervene in the governments of the Southern States, and especially to regulate the right of suffrage therein. This argument, if it did not originate with Senator Sumner, has yet been most industriously displayed by him, and in his hands has taken the form of a bill to regulate suffrage in all the States, without regard to property, race or colour.

It is strange, indeed, that a member of Congress, who claims to represent peculiarly the cultivation and scholarship of his party, and who prides himself on the abundance and accuracy of his historical illustrations, should have fallen into an errour especially deplorable for its ignorance of the commonest texts in our political annals. The school-boy even knows that, at the date of the Constitution, the States then existing were considered republican forms of government; and if Mr. Sumner had turned to his dictionary, he might readily have found that to "guarantee" means to warrant something already existing. The meaning of the clause was stated by Mr. Madison, and, writing in one of the numbers of "The Federalist," he distinctly explained that "it supposes a pre-existing government of the form which is to be guaranteed." It could have had no other meaning. In the history of the language in which it was prepared, the intent was yet more manifest; one shape of the proposition being—"that a republican constitution and its *existing* laws ought to be guaranteed to each State by the United States." The words were cut down or reduced, and with a mere verbal change consulting brevity, the proposition was accepted as it now stands—"that the United States shall guarantee to every State a republican form of government." If any doubt existed as to what was a "republican form of government," it was clearly, necessarily, to be decided by that form which each State possessed at the date of the Constitution, and which it was designed to secure as against all monarchical and aristocratical innovations.

No one then supposed, no one for eighty years following the Constitution supposed, that this clause was designed to give to Congress power to interfere with suffrage in the States, and that a restricted suffrage was to be taken for a negation of a "republican form of government." According to such a test, the governments of Virginia and Massachusetts were not republican when they came into the Union; and, indeed, all the States at that time demanded "reconstruction," as it is a remarkable fact that in all of them age, residence, sex and a property qualification, were required of electors. Indeed, according to this, even the Constitution of the United States would not be a republican form of government, since it possesses no power over the elective franchise, and, on the contrary, leaves it to be regulated by the governments subordinate to itself—the States. The only clause of the Constitution which relates at all to the subject of suffrage is that, in the choice of representatives, the electors shall have "the qualifications requisite for electors of the most numerous branch of the State Legislature." The States were left to regulate the franchise for themselves.

For eighty years the country has acquiesced in the opinion that the State governments were republican, and Congress has slept upon its supposed duty of providing for such change in the government of each State as would make it republican in the estimation of Mr. Sumner. That person has suddenly interposed to contradict the assumption of our fathers that the

States which formed the Union enjoyed republican forms of government; and proposes to interrupt their continuance in that enjoyment by admitting Congress to interfere with suffrage, even to the extent of forming a Constitution for a State! The true question, it is to be practically observed, is not whether universal suffrage may or may not be a necessary element in the republican form of government; but whether our fathers thought so, since thei ssue is as to the meaning of a particular clause in the Constitution and not as to the merit of a general proposition. And on this point, we repeat, we have the decisive rule that the design of this clause was to guarantee the existing governments of the States, none of which permitted universal suffrage.

But that question settled, the restriction of the Constitution determined, we are even not unwilling to admit to general reasoning the proposition that universal suffrage is a necessary condition of a republican government. We know, that public attention has been caught on this subject by some shallow platitudes, some "glittering generalities," about the natural rights of man to defend himself in society, and the ballot being a necessity of his political existence as a freeman. But the question is wholly mis-stated in these broad declamations of the demagogue. Some recent froth from the lips of Mr. Thaddeus Stevens is an example of what extravagances and absurdities may pass unrebuked in a senseless clamour of patriotism and vague appeals to history. In a speech in the House of Representatives, March 19, 1868, he declared: "We have reached a period when we may speak of universal suffrage, not as a boon, not as a gift, but as an inalienable right, which no man dares to take away, and which no man can surrender. His God has forbidden it; the science of government has forbidden it, and henceforth let us understand that universal suffrage operating in favour of every man who is to be governed by the votes cast, is one of those doctrines planted deeper than the granite in which our fathers laid the foundation of their immortal work—the work of universal liberty which will last just as long as that immortal doctrine shall last, and no longer"!!

The points of exclamation are our own, and are well deserved. The mistake, the wretched nonsense of Mr. Stevens is in considering as a natural, inherent right, a privilege which grows wholly out of the condition of society, and is governed by its concerns. The suffrage is conceded to those who are adjudged capable of exercising it, and this judgment is determined in the discretion of the legislative power. Those who are incapable by nature of fulfilling functions of citizenship cannot be forced to exercise them without detriment to society as well as to themselves. This is the plain rule, and is of the very frame of society. Republican governments may be more or less democratic; but it is a singular fact, that no government has ever existed in the world in which universal suffrage has prevailed! Such a government would be simply the surrender of all its worth and intelligence to an accident of numbers. In our political system, the tendency has always been to the enlargement of suffrage—a tendency the effects of which have been the corruption of elections, the lowering of the standards of public life and that evil which one of the most popular and robust of modern thinkers (John Stuart Mill) deplores as the especial affliction of America: the *raising of questions*, for the purpose of founding parties upon them. But decided as has been this tendency to extend the elective franchise, our government has judged that there were persons within the limits of its jurisdiction who were incapable of exercising all the functions of citizenship; that women, that unnaturalized foreigners, that youths of undeveloped minds should not assume as a right what from their very incapacity would be detrimental to themselves as well as to the public interest. It is of very care of them that the government keeps them in the condition of political minors. They are protected by the general intelligence and humanity of the laws; and in the case of the Negro, this protection has been assured and multiplied by special statutes, and even by a bureau solely designed for his benefit.

We are not disposed to expend argument on a truism. But there is a single consideration which cuts under the whole doctrine of universal suffrage, and which does not appear to have obtained yet the attention of the disputants. *The right to vote and the right to be voted for are equal and correlative.* If we admit the right of universal suffrage, we must annul all the qualifications to hold office. We must repeal all those various laws, Federal, State, and Municipal which require age, residence, property qualifications, etc., for public office. We must either involve ourselves in this general and ruinous license; or we must require qualifications at both ends of the line—for the voter as well as the officer. The alternative is severe, and cannot be avoided.

Upon the closest reflection, we can discover no flaw in this argument. It is as neat as it is novel. If we admit fully the right of the Negro to vote, then we cannot diminish his right to be voted for, or to ascend to any offices within the gift of the ballot. More than this, if we are to take universal suffrage as the test of "republicanism," after the school of Mr. Sumner, then we must carry the reform to the extent of nullifying all qualifications for office, such as age, residence, property, etc., and rooting from the State Constitutions an entire series of fundamental laws. These qualifications are empirical and unsound on the admission of universal suffrage, and must give way in logical sequence. A reform to this extent has probably not been practically contemplated by the Radicals in Congress; but a party which prates so much of logical necessities, and preaches the virtue of the *sequitur*, is under especial obligations to follow its doctrines to their legitimate conclusions.

Leaders of the Radical party, with professions of Negro suffrage hot in their mouths, have been sending advices to Southern Conventions that Negroes should not run for Congress, or aspire to any conspicuous office; that they should be satisfied to fill the lowest seats in political synagogues. They are to vote as much as they please, but not to be voted for. It is an insult even to the low intelligence of the Negro to abuse him thus, and make him an unrewarded instrument of the ambition of white politicians. It is a unilateral citizenship, as offensive to the instincts of justice as to the law of logic. If we are to concede universal suffrage, we must perfect it by universal license to office; it is only the first step of a reform that must proceed to universal demoralization, to the cheapening of all offices, to a wild, unrestrained, vehement competition in political life that will leave nothing good or desirable in it.

But beyond the general considerations of this doctrine of universal suffrage there is a peculiar excess in Mr. Sumner's application of it to the Southern States. It is a mockery added to absurdity, the former as arch and fiendish as the latter is flagrant and flippant. Universal suffrage means for the South Negro suffrage; and the method of enforcing it, with the preliminary conditions of martial law and other machinery of Reconstruction, is of the very essence of despotism. Whatever doubt there may be as to the meaning of a "republican form of government," it certainly and necessarily implies self-government by the people of a State; and the most adventurous dealer in political fancies would scarcely venture the assertion that the form of government dictated by Congress to accomplish Negro suffrage in the South was republican or self-government. The guaranty of a republican form of government is practically violated under pretext of its fulfillment, and is made to mean a power in Congress to impose upon a State a government that is not republican! The South is mocked, by calling the attempt to institute tyranny over her the guaranty of a republican government and by giving the name of kindness to insult and injury. This derision might at least been spared a suffering people. No device was needed. The wrong might have been done with the bold and accustomed declarations of villainy—at least without the effrontery, the brutal mockery of the highwayman who pretends a kindly and protecting care for the effects of the traveler, while rifling his pockets, and leaving him to misery and despair.

A SPECIAL CONSOLATION.

The Radical party vindicating the action of the South in the late war—A new interpretation of "Copperheads"—Speech of George H. Pendleton—Two wars since 1860: one for the Union, the other for the Constitution—President Lincoln's plea of necessity—Precedents of 1776 and 1812—Reasons for the war on the Constitution—Extract from an English publicist—Identity of the Two Rebellions, 1776 and 1861—Extraordinary declaration of President Johnson—Prophecy of the "lost cause regained."

Regarding the chain of unconstitutional acts which Congress has accomplished since the war, there is one great consolatory idea for the South, which scarcely appears to have been developed in the current commentaries of the press. It is the logical, inevitable tendency of such proceedings to vindicate the past war; to suggest that constitutional liberty was really in issue in it, since the Republican party has made such use of its success, and the victors have unmasked such opinions and purposes; and, finally, to exhibit the South, instead of fighting in an odious rebellion, engaged in a noble and admirable contest, not unlike that of 1776. This idea was imperfectly apprehended in the war, but now obtains fuller exposition, a more complete developement in the political sequel. There were men during the war loosely called "Copperheads," whose inclination to the South was much more intelligent than the ordinary sympathies with that combatant; who had obtained the idea that, independently of the issue of the Union, was a great, underlying struggle of constitutional law and traditional liberty, and that Robert E. Lee, in that sense, was fighting his battles for the North, as well as for the South! This idea was far above the vulgar recriminations of party, the common reproach of disloyality, "secession proclivities, etc.;" it was harboured by a few intelligent persons, who indignantly repelled the charge of community of sentiment with Secessionists and Southern sympathizers, and constantly asserted their attachment to the Union, along with their dissent from the Republican party.

These men were misunderstood by both sections; and the author well recollects how confused were the regards of the South for War Democrats of the McClellan and Pendleton school. But their idea has recently been enlightened; and thoughtful men have already discovered that the past war had the significance of a political revolution, as well as that of a specific contest for the Union. Every historical crisis has its particular occasion, and the tendency of the common mind is to dwell on this occasion, to occupy itself with the mere visible outward event. Thus in the late war there were many who concerned themselves wholly for the Union, and sunk every other consideration in anxiety for its restoration. They did not conceive that superiour significance of the contest, that is now so apparent; they did not understand that the constitutional liberty of the whole country was imperiled; they did not understand that, going on under the forms of rebellious arms, there was a continuation of the great political struggle of 1776.

When George H. Pendleton* of Ohio stood in conspicuous opposition in Congress to its series of war measures, he concluded one of his orations with this fine burst of eloquence:—"When your work shall be accomplished, when our Constitu-

* With reference to this remarkable representative of the Democratic party during the war, the author has nad recent occasion in a biographical article to describe his political opinions.

"The chief historical interest of Mr. Pendleton's life attaches to his course in Congress during the late war, wherein he was the conspicuous representative of a class or division

tion is dead, when our liberties are gone, when our Government is destroyed, when these States—no longer held secure in their proper position by the power of our matchless Constitution, so that they emulate in accordant action the stars, as by the divine decree they encircle in their mysterious courses the foot-stool of the eternal throne, and extract from the harmony of conflicting elements the true music of the spheres—shall have given place to States discordant, dissevered, belligerent, to a land rent with civil feuds, and drenched in fratricidal blood, history will hold its dread inquest, and in the presence of appalled humanity will render judgment, that base and degenerate children, deserting the teachings of their fathers, deserting the teaching of the past, departing from the ways of pleasantness and peace, rebelling against the wisdom and be-

of opinion that has suffered much from misrepresentation, and that claims a peculiar and searching review. It was then the convenient fashion of the Republican party to call all who dissented from them, "Copperheads," and under this venomous term aggregate all the elements of opposition. The classification was as illogical as it was violent; for it cannot escape the candid judgment that the grounds of dissent from the policy of the Republicans in the past war were of the most various character. There were those who sympathized with the South in a sectional sense; there were others, who were merely compassionate, and while admitting the South to be in errour thought her hardly and cruelly punished; there were sentimentalists and humanitarians; but apart from all these was a distinct, firm, intelligent party, which, asserting the inviolability of the Union, and voting men and means to vindicate it, was yet constantly for separating the war from an attempt upon the Constitution, and drawing the line between an appeal to arms for a specific issue and a political revolution involving the laws and traditions of the country. The ground of this party was very high; it suffered reproach, North and South, from misrepresentation; but it is to be remarked that the intelligent men of the South during the war, valued its dissent from the reigning policy at Washington much more than open protestations of sympathy from another class of "Copperheads," in proportion as it was more intelligent, more permanent, and even more effective, because more moderate, in vindication of the principles which rested at the bottom of the contest."

"'The Union' was serviceable, as the outward event or occasion usually is in any historical crisis, to inspire the populace and seize its imagination. Mr. Pendleton acknowledged this inspiration; he knew and confessed the value of the Union; but he was unwilling in contesting it to assault the Constitution; he saw that Lincoln and his party were "running the machine" in the double groove of a political revolution; and he proposed, however ineffectually, to confine the war to its avowed objects, and to contain it as far as possible within the limits of the Constitution. This is the whole explanation of his course in Congress."

neficence of the Almighty, with hearts filled with pride, and souls stained with fanaticism and passion, struck the matricidal blow, and at the same moment indignant and outraged Heaven wreaked upon them the just retribution of their terrible and nameless crime."

Briefly, there were those who had a realization of two wars—the war against the Union and the war against the Constitution. The attempt to conceal the latter was this wretched argument: that the infringements on the Constitution were mere affairs of necessity in the war, that there was no design upon that instrument, further than some temporary violations, to impart an extraordinary vigour to hostilities. We give this argument in its best shape in a notable declaration made by President Lincoln, in 1864:—"I felt that measures, otherwise unconstitutional, might become lawful by becoming *indispensable* to the preservation of the Constitution, through the preservation of the nation." The fallacy captivated the vulgar; but to the intelligent it was a dogma as violent, as it was shallow. They recognized the "indispensable means" suggested by the party in power as a sum of despotism: the extinction of liberty, of free speech, of free press, of free ballot, of jury trial, of *habeas corpus*; the subjection of private property to arbitrary seizure and confiscation; the practice of arbitrary arrest and imprisonment, secret trial and punishment; the violation of private contracts by "legal tender" laws; the erection of a huge system of conscription; the passage of *ex post facto* laws and bills of attainder; the supremacy of the military over the civil power.

Was this despotic machinery necessary to carry on the war, or was it something apart from it, a distinct concern? Happily, the American people had had two great wars preceding

5*

that of 1861—the war of 1776 and of 1812; and it could not but occur to the recollections of those persons who had any knowledge of history, that in neither of these had the Government found it necessary to adopt any of the measures referred to by the modern Republican party as indispensable in a state of war. Mr. Jefferson declared as the great merit of Washington that he "scrupulously obeyed the laws during his whole career, civil and military." An equal encomium is due Madison. Both Presidents had conducted the nation through great and critical wars; but neither had ever suspended the civil law, or claimed, under any supposed necessity, to exercise unconstitutional rights, or even attempted to punish, without the ordinary forms of law, a single citizen not attached to the military service!

Against the dogma of Mr. Lincoln were here two high precedents—the highest in American history. Against this same dogma was an unbroken current of judicial decisions, the compact authority of all lessons of ancestral wisdom. "The spirit of liberty," said Mr. Webster, "will not permit power to overstep its prescribed limits, though good intent, patriotic intent, come along with it. This is the nature of constitutional liberty. This is our liberty." Under this enlightenment it is not strange that reflecting men should have pierced the fallacy of Abraham Lincoln and his party, and apprehended in the disguise a new and dangerous movement. It was, in truth, a movement of a second war, conducted under the cloak of the first, and aimed at the most vital parts of the Constitution.

The apprehension of this revolutionary design was strongly felt from 1861 to 1865. But the particular thought we wish to bring to the reader is, that since the war there has been in the conduct of the Republican party such additional evidence of the truth of the apprehension as to confirm it, and to constitute it a positive conviction. That conduct, indeed, reveals how intelligent was the original opposition to this party; how just and significant was the war, at least so far as it was directed against its pretensions. It is the spectacle of a party furnishing, in the sequel, the conclusive evidence of its original concealed wickedness. If any doubt had lingered as to the extent of that party's designs, if some minds had been captivated by its plea of necessity, the suspense or delusion no longer exists. Now when there occur such new distinct evidences of unconstitutional and revolutionary purposes manifested by Congress, taking place since the war has ceased, since its plea of necessity no longer operates, since there are no longer tolerable excuses or decent disguises, since a permanent policy has taken the place of a professed expediency, and plain deliberation has ensued upon passion, surely no judicious mind can longer be in ignorance of the true character and meaning of the past war, or fail to perceive that it contained a stake larger than that of the Union.

We are left to the supposition that there was really a historical and logical necessity to operate on the Republican party, and to continue after the war its display of hostility to the Constitution; and it is in the discovery of this necessity, we are persuaded, that we have a consistent explanation of the present situation at Washington and of the real issues of the past war. This party, on its original mission against Slavery, had started on the theory of Consolidation; and having abolished Slavery, we find it now obeying the force of a long political education, and moved by the supreme concern of prolonging its existence as a party, in maintaining a condition of general hostility to the Constitution. When a party has conceived a sentiment of revolution, it will easily find or make occasions through which to develope it, and to renew its leases of power. The difficulty of particular questions is soon supplied; and the common mistake of the popular mind is in limiting to these questions the designs of party. It is thus a number of superficial and amiable politicians of the South have mistaken the situation at Washington; have advised a policy of concessions, when every concession has been the signal of a new demand; and have imagined that they have only to appease a temporary rage of party, when the necessity is really to answer the demands of a persistent and fast-progressing revolution.

This revolution is older and broader than the war, that was its recent incident. The rebellion of 1861 had its immediate question in the preservation of the Union; but beyond there might well reside a paramount issue of constitutional liberty. There is no violence in such a supposition. The lesson of history is that, for whatever immediate objects rebellions have been kindled, the ultimate fruit, in case of success, is a larger share of public liberty. It has been observed that it is the peculiar lot of the Anglo-Saxon race to win their freedom by rebellion, and to preserve it by rebellion. No matter what may first excite the popular revolt, it is remarked that it obtains significance as it progresses, and that the movement naturally ascends to a war for liberty. The war of 1776 demanded ostensibly nothing more than separation from Great Britain; that was its particular occasion and object; and if confined to that alone, as Alexander Hamilton and a large party in the North insisted, its success would have been a very inconsiderable affair, nothing more than the commonplace in history of a change of rulers, the event of a dynasty. But Mr. Jefferson, in the Declaration of Independence, dated even with it a political revolution; and it instantly possessed a new significance, became a large and important contest for liberty.

We have referred to the continuation or renewal of that contest, in 1861. It is a fruitful thought: the profound identity of the Two Rebellions, 1776 and 1861. Such identities are the discoveries and studies of the philosophic historian. Indeed, the suggestions we have just made, have been quickened by a recent English author (Mr. Morley) who, in a political study of Edmund Burke and his times, remarks that the American Rebellion of 1776, so far from involving only the tenure of the colonies, was logically and historically a part of the great constitutional struggle commenced in 1760, and effectually decided it. What he says of this is so parallel to what we are considering, that we may introduce it here for the benefit of the reader—

"It is almost demonstrably certain that the vindication of the supremacy of popular interests over all other considerations would have been bootless toil, and that the great constitutional struggle, from 1760 to 1783, would have ended otherwise than it did, but for the failure of the war against the insurgent colonies and the final establishment of American independence. It was this portentous transaction which finally routed the arbitrary and despotic pretensions of the House of Commons over the people, which put an end to the hopes entertained by the sovereign of making his personal will supreme in the chambers, and which established the principle of Cabinet as distinguished from Departmental responsibility. Fox might well talk of the early royalist victory in the war as the terrible news from Rhode Island. The struggle which began successfully at Brentford, in Middlesex, was continued at Boston, in Massachusetts. The scene had changed, but the conflicting principles were the same. The defeat and subjugation of the colonists would have been followed by the final annihilation of the opposition in the mother country. The War of Independence was virtually a second English civil war. The ruin of the American cause would have been also the ruin of the constitutional cause in England; and a patriotic Englishman may revere the memory of Patrick Henry and George Washington not less justly than the patriotic American."

So the time may come, when the patriotic American may render his thanks to Davis and Lee for efforts which, once disesteemed as the act of rebellion, may hereafter be enlightened as parts of a great constitutional struggle. It is not a strained thought in the light of what the Republican party is now doing, in the imprudence of victory, to confess its real idea and purpose in the war, and to execute its consequences. There is a remarkable passage in a message of President Johnson to Congress, which comes in just here, fitting to the extract from Mr. Morley, and completing the thought which we have proposed for the meditation of the intelligent:—

"Those who advocated the right of Secession alleged in their own justification that we had no regard for law, and that their rights of property, life, and liberty would not be safe under the Constitution as administered by us. If we now verify their assertion, we prove that they were in truth and in fact fighting for their liberty, and, instead of branding their leaders with the dishonouring names of traitors against a righteous and legal Government, we elevate them in history to the rank of self-sacrificing patriots, consecrate them to the admiration of the world, and place them by the side of Washington, Hampton and Sydney!"

It is when this new illumination of the war shall take place that we shall approach the full realization of "The Lost Cause Regained;" when its leaders shall be raised to admiration, its memories restored to honour, and its great names inscribed in a new Pantheon of patriotic adoration. Every unconstitutional act of Congress is logically and irreparably directed to such a consummation. It is a new thought; a new animation for the

South; a new prophecy of "The Lost Cause Regained;" a new meditation in the confused strife and turmoil of the day. Surely the people of the South will be better able to support the oppression and outrage of their present rulers, when they reflect that these are effectively, though unconsciously, working out their vindication, and that the blind guide of party is steadily conducting them to that bar of history where the past "rebels" are to be proclaimed the true patriots.

III.

THE NEGRO QUESTION.

RETROSPECT OF SLAVERY

The political question of the Negro resolved to one of natural history—Value of the fact of the specific inferiourity of the Negro—Its importance in a retrospect of the sectional controversy and war—The tribute of history to Negro Slavery in the South—The equality doctrine of the Declaration of Independence, so far from condemning Slavery, obtained from the contact and influence of it—The true and *only* defence of Slavery—Mistakes of Southern politicians—Their appeal to the Constitution in behalf of Slavery, a mean and infamous one—The important premise of the entire Slavery Question, the inferiourity of the Negro.

Congress appeared, some months ago, disposed to give some attention to ethnological and scientific inquiries on the subject of the Negro. It could not have been better employed, for after all, the whole political controversy about the son of Ham is contained in the question, whether he is a mere variety of the human race, measurably capable of equality with its highest developments, or a distinct, inferiour species of man, doomed by the inexorable laws of nature to certain limits and conditions of existence. In short, the political question of the Negro, resolved to its last elements, is simply and purely a question of natural history, for it is at last by the the standards of nature that we are to determine, whether the Radical task of Negro equality is practicable, or a violent and impossible experiment, sure as all experiments against nature are, to recoil upon and punish itself.

We believe, indeed, that the specific, permanent inferiourity of the Negro, so far from being a mere disputation of the learned, a scholastic entertainment, is, as discovered and eviscerated by the past war, the most important question of modern times, and one vital to the whole body of American civilization. This question once determined, we enlighten the whole past controversy of Slavery; we occupy the one ultimate logical foundation of the entire perplexed argument on this subject, with all its forms, syllogisms and expressions; and we secure for the future affairs of the country an intelligent rule of action. If, as it now appears, we have the settled prospect that the white man and the Negro, under certain circumstances, which will be elsewhere discussed, shall exist in juxtaposition, then a specific knowledge of this black race, and its relations to our own, may truly be declared a vital and transcendent consideration, connected with our national destiny, and involving questions not second in importance to any that have ever been presented to a civilized and Christian people.

The value of the fact of the Negro's inferiourity is very great. We repeat that it furnishes the key to much that is past in the sectional controversy of North and South. It is with respect to this single fact that we design a brief retrospect of Slavery, rather than to renew the "vexed question," the comparative enumeration of virtues and vices. The intelligent Southerner of this day is satisfied to leave this controversy to the future historian; assured that whatever of vices and defects he may ascribe to Slavery, he cannot omit its contributions in the past;

that he cannot fail to write on the broad, judicial pages of the nation's record in civilization and progress, that Slavery developed the vast regions south of the Ohio, giving to the world cheap cotton, sugar and rice; that it produced nearly all the materials of foreign export; that furnishing two hundred millions of annual exports from the South, it supplied the nutriment of national commerce, besides a bountiful market for the reward of the commercial and manufacturing industry of the North; that, whatever theorists may allege, it stimulated the republican ideas of the white population, to the extent of producing the most liberal statesmen in America, and contributing the larger portion of the great Democratic party; and that it created that most curious party alliance in our political history—the capital of the South and the labour of the North—which has governed the country with peculiar honour and most memorable renown.

These are historical facts of great breadth. We promised to confine ourselves to the single question of the Negro's inferiourity. It really attaches to what we have just written; and the value of the fact of that inferiourity is most apparent, most striking in the last enumeration of the effects of Slavery. The thoughtful historian of America will find that the obvious visible inferiourity of the Negro was constantly, although unconsciously, educating the people of the South to a disregard of the mere artificial distinctions of society, by the side of this great natural difference of races—was, in fact, developing, by a process of comparison, the idea of equality as among men of the same race; and he may startle some convictions when he announces the important political discovery that the equality clause of the Declaration of Independence, so far from condemning Negro Slavery, was obtained from it, originated in its contact and experience! It is a startling declaration in our political history, a vivacious interjection; yet it is profoundly true. Mr. Jefferson's doctrine of equality as of men of the same race was merely the transfer to the domain of politics of that law of natural history which teaches us that all *the members of a species are equal.* The varieties within the boundaries of a single species are of no account in comparison with the differences as between distinct species. The habitual observation of the South was as between two species or races of men; and there was an obvious mental necessity that as people regarded this great natural distinction, they should attach less importance to those inferiour distinctions made by society in mere classes and conditions of life, and thus progress to clearer perceptions of the natural equality of their own species and race. It is thus that the Negro Slavery of the South became the instructor of white republicanism; that the inferiourity of the Negro is to be recognized as a fruitful and conservative principle in our system of politics; and that we claim a value for this fact, which we suggested at the beginning of this article would exceed the ordinary estimates.

We add another view of the importance of this fact. The permanent, natural inferiourity of the Negro was the true and *only* defence of Slavery. The intelligence of the South has at last awaked to this idea in the stimulating light of the recent war and its consequences; but it is strange how in the past the Southern mind wandered in its defences of Slavery, and chose the narrowest and most imperfect grounds for a controversy which it might have maintained on an impregnable principle of natural law.* The question of races figured slightly in the

* Of the imperfect and confused notions of Negro Slavery on the part of the wisest politicians of the South, a striking example is afforded by Thomas Jefferson. He saw what all candid and humane men saw, that Slavery was liable to abuses, and his compassion

accustomed debate and was thought to be scarcely more than a nice and curious philosophy. The argument *a posteriori* was preferred to that *a priori*; and the advocates of Slavery were generally content to point to its effects, to its maintenance in profound peace without military machinery, to its fruits of industry, to its evidences of benevolence. Such reasoning was more suggestive than convincing; but more imperfect yet was the common argument that the defence of Slavery was assured by the guaranties of Constitutional law, and that, without reference to moral questions, it had a secure lodging in the Consti-

was moved by frequent incidents of cruelty to the Negro, committed with impunity, through looseness of the law, or the licenses of public sentiment in particular neighbourhoods. A remedy was needed.

Before the war the author had meditated a great missionary effort for the unification of all laws touching the Negro; for a code which should exhibit all possible humanity, and allow all possible liberty to the Negro, consistent with the single fact of compulsory service; which should have the effect of enlightening the world as to the true nature of the "peculiar institution" of the South, and especially vindicating it from the censure attaching to the misnomer, "slavery"—a libel of party nomenclature. It was a large, inspiring work, worthy of the greatest minds. The war interrupted it. Yet the author cannot help believing to this day that the remedy proposed—ameliorating the condition of the Negro and advertising, in the form of public laws, his true condition to the world—would have satisfied the sympathies of the intelligent, and answered all reasonable demands of the humane.

The mistake of Mr. Jefferson was in jumping to Emancipation, and seeing no remedy for existing evils short of it. The design, the sentiment was good; but the remedy proposed was mistaken and excessive, and betrayed an ignorance of the fundamental idea of Slavery, and a misconception of the true wants of the Negro scarcely to be expected in a mind like that of Jefferson. Yet, however Mr. Jefferson was carried away by a sentimental fervour, and desired for the Negro the gift of Emancipation, he was yet thoroughly convinced that the released black could never live on terms of equality with the white man in the same political community. The Anti-Slavery party has quoted from this great authority with ingenious partiality and unfairness, and has invariably omitted the words which recoil on their policy. If Jefferson was an Emancipationist, he was yet far from being an Abolitionist in the modern sense of the term. We can, indeed, add nothing to the perspicuity or emphasis of the following words of the Sage of Monticello: "Nothing is more clearly written in the book of destiny than the emancipation of the blacks; and it is equally certain that the two races will never live in state of equal freedom under the same government, so insurmountable are the barriers which nature, habits and opinions have established between them."

We may add the remarkable fact that of all leading men in the South who ever at any time desired Emancipation, not one failed to couple it with the condition that the Negro should be colonized, or withdrawn from competition with the white man; and in this respect they have been invariably misquoted by the Anti-Slavery party of the North. *Suppressio veri, suggestio falsi.*

tution of the United States. Of what avail was this refuge when the devotees of Anti-Slavery, in the language of one of their eloquent leaders were prepared to "rend the Union to destroy Slavery, though hedged round by the triple bars of the national compact, and though thirty-three crowned sovereigns with arms in their hands stood around it!" How dull must have been the statesmanship of the South that did not perceive the lesson running through all history, that laws, whether organic or statute, avail nothing against the steady encroachment of a moral sentiment, and that where a people has once fully satisfied itself that an evil is to be corrected, it will move upon it by whatever means are most direct and decisive!

The defence of Slavery by virtue of the Constitution was essentially narrow and infamously mean. It amounted to scarcely more than the plea so often made in criminal courts for the ingenious villain: that a crime has been committed, but there is no law to reach it, and the offence is to escape on a technicality. The true question in Negro Slavery was that of right or wrong. It was all wrong, if the Negro was really the equivalent of the white man enveloped in a black skin. Admit this and Slavery becomes a great crime; the breach of the Constitution to attack it, a sacrifice of virtue and patriotism; the war to exterminate it, a rightful one; the consequent policy of Negro equality, just; the gift of the suffrage, unavoidable; and even rewards of the Negro above the white man and a superiour solicitude for him, commendable in view of his deprivations and sufferings in the past. We cannot stop in the argument; it runs irresistibly to every extremity of the governing Radical policy at Washington, and surrenders every question in the present political controversy. We must do—what the South has never fairly done—meet the whole controversy at the minor premise, contending for the natural inferiourity of the Negro. It is from this inferiourity that we deduce all the benefits of Slavery in the past. It is from this inferiourity that we draw all our arguments with respect to future experiments on the Negro. The fact is important as a historical vindication of the past. It is also important as a supreme instruction for the future.

It will be well now to summon the evidences of a fact so important and to secure at once what we esteem the most pregnant and fruitful premise in all the political controversies of our day.

INFERIOURITY OF THE NEGRO.

The Scientific Argument—Divisions of the organic world—Qualities of a "Species"—The law of hybridity—The Negro, the base of the *generic column* of Man—No genus without species—Limits of interunion between Negroes and Whites—The Octoroon absolutely sterile—Uniformity of the type of the Negro—The excavations of Champollion—*The Religious Argument*—Hypothesis of a Divine miracle with reference to the Negro—*The Historic Argument*—The Negro in Africa—Former civilization of the Nile—A glance at Liberia—The idea of the inferiourity of the Negro, one of benevolence.

We propose to make a brief summary of the evidences of the inferiourity of the Negro, as a distinct race of men. The subject has occupied many large volumes; but we shall dispatch it here in a limited space, putting it in a form for easy popular apprehension, and in a shape as orderly and compact as possible.

1. *The Scientific Argument.* We are taught by science that the organic world consists of different forms and orders, subject to many subdivisions; that those groups of beings are in a certain sense independent systems, worlds in themselves—such being the grand economy of nature that one or more of them might be utterly extinguished (as in fact we are informed by geologists has been the case with many forms of animals, and perhaps of man too) without interrupting the course and harmony of the universe. The aggregate world would yet live and move without them. These divisions of being are founded on differences in form and character, at intervals which regularly diminish until they come down to "varieties" of the same creature. The organic world is thus divided into classes, orders, genera, species and varieties. The last are distinguished only by accidental circumstances and are more or less permanent, as these circumstances operate. The quality of the *species* is that its members, while equal to each other, differ from those of other species, ascending or descending, to the extent that one degree never passes into another; and its test is that the principle of interunion is limited, that while different species may be capable of interunion, it is only to a limited extent, the product ultimately perishing by the inexorable law of *hybridity*, by which nature punishes the transgression of her laws. The relations of these species to each other is that of gradual improvement or ascent; that is, taking the number of species of which a genus is composed, we find the one next above the lowest with all the qualities of the latter, but with fuller developement, more elaborate organization, and with corresponding faculties of a higher order. In other words, there is a head and a base to the generic column. It begins with the lowest or simplest formation, and rises in the scale of being until it is completed;

and while these formations *generically* considered resemble each other, yet *specifically* considered, they are absolutely distinct, unlike each other in everything, to the minutest particle of elementary matter.

In Man we find the Negro as the base of the generic column; and ascending, in order, the different races above him—the Esquimaux, the Aboriginal American, the Malay or Oceanic, the Mongolian—we at last reach in the Caucasian or the *historic* race the perfection of the highest form of the human creation. The Great Creator has impressed on all his works evidences of limitless conception and power. Everywhere in nature we discover the principle of variety attesting the multitude, the infinity of creative design. It would be strange, indeed, if in Man alone, the perfection of the Creator's works and His crowning glory, this principle should be omitted; that in him of all other beings there should be manifested poverty of creative design; that in him, of the whole animal creation, there should be presented the contradiction and anomaly of *a genus without species!* In the entire world of animal existence there is no such fact as a single species. Thus, those who insist that the human creation is composed of a single species contradict or ignore the most constant, universal and uniform fact in organic life. They violate the whole order and analogy of Nature in insisting that Man is incapable of specific divisions of being; they deny the great law of adaptation, signifying Divine Providence, in supposing that Man, who inhabits the whole range of organic and animal life, partakes of none of its relations and laws, and furnishes in himself the single instance of but one type and capacity amid so many changes. Rightly estimating the power of different evidences, there is none higher or nobler, none in closer converse with the Divine intelligence than that drawn from Analogy. It is this, beyond all other arguments, which secures the proof of different species of Man. He can be no exception to the designs of the Creator; and the law that distributes all created being, and runs the lines of specific differences through the whole animal world must apply to him.

But it has been said that the test of different species, as we have designated it above, does not apply to the Negro—that *the principle of interunion* between him and the white man is not limited, and that therefore they are but "varieties" which may approach and assimilate by the operation of circumstances. It was seen that white men cohabited with Negro women and that the offspring in turn reproduced itself; wherefore it was argued that they were but varieties with all powers of virility as between themselves, for if they had been different species, the mulatto would have been as incapable of reproduction, as the mule, the offspring of the horse and ass, is. But the argument is short and deficient; for the fact is that although the mulatto reproduces, this power is diminished in each generation where he intermarries with other hybrids, until at last it is utterly lost and the progeny becomes absolutely sterile. It has been asserted, as the result of some recent scientific investigations, that this conclusion of sterility occurs in the *fourth* generation; but wherever does occur the natural barrier of this exceptional form of being, it is sufficient for the purposes of our argument to know that it does occur somewhere; that at some period absolute sterility intervenes, that the principle of interunion is *limited*, no matter to what degree of limitation. It may be in the light of these facts that the difference between the white man and the Negro is not as great as between some other species of animals; but that this difference is *specific* is sufficiently proved from the fact that the law of hybridity *does* control the offspring, although it may be in a comparatively distant generation, and that there is an ultimate and absolute barrier beyond which "mulattoism" cannot exist. The question is as to the degree, not as to the nature of the difference. We know that the offspring of the white man and the Negro is essentially hybrid; that "mulattoism" is absolutely confined to a limited number of generations, its virile power decreasing at each effort of reproduction; and the reason that we are not familiar with the conclusion of this exceptional offspring in absolute sterility is, that its destruction is worked out through constitutional fragility and limited longevity as much, perhaps, as through imperfect capacity of reproduction.

But in addition to these arguments of science for the distinct and inferiour race of the Negro—in addition to what Analogy proclaims of the law of order, and to what investigation asserts of the experiment of interunion—we have those visible and tangible evidences of the difference between the white and black man, which furnish the argument best suited for popular appreciation, and determine the question by the irresistible force of the senses. It was likely for naturalists who lived some centuries ago, and who scarcely knew anything of the human creation beyond the two hundred millions of Caucasians in Europe, to suppose that there was but one species of man, and that those who inhabited distant and unexplored parts of the world were like themselves, except in the operation and effect of the circumstances which surrounded them. It is even possible for those in modern times, who know nothing about the Negro except that he has a black skin, to take hold of the superficial imagination that he is merely "a coloured man," and raising the cry of "no distinction of colour" to dash at once into the dogmas of equality. But those who have a clear and more intimate knowledge of the Negro; who know the uniform facts attaching to his existence; who in their ordinary experience have seen Negro parents having Negro offspring, as Indians have Indian offspring, and whites have white offspring, "each after its kind" regularly and invariably as in other forms of existence; and who fortifying these common daily observations by the lesson of history, that thus it has been in all kinds of climate and all kinds of circumstances, without change or symptom of change, regardless of the fact that the Negro may have lived four thousand years ago or yesterday, may have been "free or slave," may have basked on the sands of Africa, or may have produced his offspring amid the snows of Canada, can never be persuaded by any amount of reasoning that he is not a Negro as surely as the crow is a crow and not a dove, that he is specifically different from themselves, and that nothing short of a Divine miracle can assimilate him to the lordly type of the Caucasian, the master-man of the world!

It is not the mere, unimportant difference of colour. It is a difference, as science teaches us, through the whole anatomical detail, including all the organs, tissues and systems down to the minutest atom of the bodily structure. It is not necessary to go through these details here; for there is enough outwardly and obviously apparent of the specific differences of the Negro to determine the judgment of any mind capable of reasoning from cause to effect. We see these differences as well as that of colour in the *tout ensemble* of the anatomical formation of the Negro; in the small average of his brain; in his inclination to the quadruped posture; in the shape of the pelvis; in the hair, *sui generis* and triangular in shape; in the features flat, shapeless and indistinct, the sunken nose, the enormous lips, the receding forehead, the sodden animal aspect, with its limited and coarse ranges of expression. Looking at these marks we have only to apply the natural law, that the outward differences must have their counterparts in the inward structure, to apprehend the conclusion that the Negro differs from the white man in the minutest atom of elementary matter, and to believe, what the microscope of the man of science reveals, that even a single globule of his blood differs from that of the white man as widely as the colour, hair, or other outward quality that confronts our daily observation.

And so it has been for four thousand years. It is within comparatively recent times that a new aid has been summoned to History, a new avenue of information opened into the mysteries of the past by the labours of the excavator in the scenes of ancient story. It is in the light of these astonishing revelations—such as those of the celebrated Champollion—that we discover the specific character of the Negro forty centuries ago with absolute and unmistakable certainty as the same displayed to the eyes of the present generation—the same in structure and features, presenting the same marked differences from the Caucasian race which we observe to-day and which have accompanied every generation under every condition of circumstances, of climate, social condition, education, time and accident.* It is but one step more in the argument—and that obvious and natural—to assert that what

* These facts, even putting aside the theory of the Negro as a distinct "species" of man, yet show him such a "*permanent* variety" as to answer all the ends of the argument; that his inferiourity is such as to exclude the prospect of his advancement to equality with the white man, and to assign him to the condition of a subordinate creature. Indeed, in view of these facts, it is not necessary to assert the inferiourity of the Negro as a quality of the *species*, if it attaches so permanently to him even as a *variety* of the race of man. This observation, although sunk to the place of a foot-note,

has existed uniform and undeviating in the course of four thousand years must have been so from the beginning, and have proceeded from the hand of the Great Creator. If the Negro in this long time, these past ages, has preserved his integrity, and transmitted to each succeeding generation the exact and complete type of himself, we must suppose that thus he existed in the anteriour period and that thus he will continue in future time—specifically and hopelessly inferiour to the white man.

2. *The Religious Argument.* But after all that science has demonstrated on this subject, we have a certain Biblical argument, which it has become recently fashionable to interpose as against the doctrine of distinct races, and which has frequently silenced discussion by a dogma as arrogant in tone as it is puerile in character. It is said that the inspired narration in the book of Genesis, showing all men descended from a single pair in the garden of Eden, secures the doctrine of the unity of races, and that it is forbidden and impious for science to allege to the contrary. This argument may be dispatched by a single consideration. Even if we are to accept the story in Genesis as literally and scientifically correct, it does not

is *very important*, as it silences the advocates of Negro equality on either of the two suppositions which the case admits.

Such discoveries as those of Champollion, *at least*, furnish the visible evidence of a *permanence* in the variety of the Negro, which, if it does not render naturally and absolutely impossible the doctrine of his equality with the white man, yet postpones it to a period beyond all reasonable calculation in human legislation, and makes it a mere phantom of the imagination. Four thousand years look down upon Congress! In all that time the Negro, whether a "species" or a "variety," has been marked, as he is to-day, an inferiour man; and that, after forty centuries, in which the integrity of the type has been faithfully preserved, it is to be instantly and radically changed, and the Negro make a sudden apparition as the equal and rival of the Caucasian, is rather too much for any human credulity. The interval is too vast, the "variety" too "permanent" for any effect of equality within any appreciable time; it is an indefinite, if not an infinite progression, *ad astra*, beyond the reach of mortal calculation.

exclude the possibility or even probability that God may not have thereafter worked a *miracle*—as He did at Babel in the division of tongues—and have separated the races of men as well by different natures as by different tongues and impossible distances. Every sincere believer in Christianity is estopped from denying the supposition of such a miracle. The whole Christian religion is founded on miracles; they are a machinery which the true believer admits on even slight occasions—why not then in this great matter of the Divine economy? If it be contended that God *at any time* might not establish the distinction of races, we limit His power and insult His majesty; and no less crime of impiety than this is committed by those who insist, that the Almighty Creator could have regulated this matter of races at no other time than on "the seventh day" of creation, and in no other place than in the garden of Eden. But the argument is not worth pursuit; it runs at last into derogation of the Divine Power; and we are satisfied to believe that, if as science and all human arguments lead us to suppose, the creature Man has been divided into different races, it was so by the will of the Almighty without any limitations of time and place within which to perform the greatest or the least of His works.

3. *The Historic Argument.* The little we know of the Negro historically is fatal to his claim of similar nature and possible equality with the white man. We find him in all known records of the world incapable of improvement, alien to progress, an incorrigible straggler from the march of civilization; if we may except what improvement he has obtained from the condition of so called slavery in America, where his special endowment of the *imitative* faculty has been called and con-

strained into unusual exercise by virtue of his inferiour position. But apart from this exceptional and limited civilization he has obtained from the contact of a white master, which grows out of the narrow faculty of imitation, and exists only within the boundaries of a certain association, the Negro remains in Africa a stationary barbarian, or exists in other countries, a hopeless retrograde. For four thousand years he has remained within the prison-house of African barbarism; and although great empires have been planted upon his borders and the *foci* of enlightenment have been erected around him—although countless myriads of white men have lived and died on the soil of Africa, and vast populations and entire nations have emigrated to that continent with the lights of civilization—the Negro has never yet been permanently affected by the contact, and the light that has shone upon his condition has only made the darkness more visible. The noble civilization in the valley of the Nile, which followed the Christian era, and at one time boasted forty thousand inmates of religious houses within its boundaries, has perished and left not a trace upon the Negro who lived in view of its splendid structures and came within the influences of its religious missions. So, too, the modern experiment of Liberia has utterly failed in its mission of civilization, and, by the candid confessions of those who have made sincere and unwearied contributions to it, has only succeeded in putting out a picket line of *trading posts* on the borders of a hostile and repellant barbarism. The Negro within the Tropical dominion remains what he was many centuries ago; implacable to the advances of civilization, or susceptible only to the vices which follow in its train. As long as he has been known to history, he has performed no part in it. He is incapable of transmitting knowledge; he has never invented an alphabet, or even a system of numerals; he is invariably found without any rudiments of cultivation originated by himself, and therefore essays without effect the higher stages of progress. Civilization finds no foundation to work upon in him; and what he obtains, even temporarily or in the slightest degree from its contact, is empirical and perishes with the surrounding circumstances.

A condition, such as this, must rest on permanent and well-defined causes. It fitly completes and closes the evidence of the specific, permanent, irrevocable inferiourity of the Negro —an inferiourity capable, it is true, of a degree of advance and developement in exceptional circumstances (as in the condition of servitude and its tendency to copy), but otherwise and ultimately hopeless, the only possible margin of improvement existing within limits fixed and determinate, beyond which the Negro can no more progress than he can alter the colour of his skin or the form of his brain.*

The value of this fact—which we shall take as proved by the summary of arguments above—we have already referred to. So far from being a barren speculation, we repeat, it involves some of the most important problems of politics and society. It establishes the true *status* of the Negro; it decides his proper relations to the white man; it determines the measure of his limited improvement or comparative civilization; it indicates the proper schools of that civilization. So far from being offensive to humanity, it solicits for the Negro the truest philanthropy, the most intelligent and effective kindness; for the recognition of his inferiourity does not diminish, but multiplies his claims on an intelligent benevolence, and would take him from a false condition to put him in the place that fits his nature, suits his qualities, and therefore consults his happiness.

IV.

THE TRUE HOPE OF THE SOUTH

CONDITION AND TEMPER OF THE SOUTHERN PEOPLE.

The black thread of the Negro in the web of party—Division of the Anti-Slavery party into Abolitionists and Negrophilists—Union of these two parties in Reconstruction—A new and enlarged edition of the "*Irrepressible Conflict*"—The proposition of Negro Suffrage scouted in the North—Elections of 1867 in Ohio, Minnesota, Kansas and New Jersey—The homogeneousness and political identity of the nation risked by the Negro—A curious comparison by B. F. Butler between the Negro and an unfortunate beast—The ballot, a fatal gift for the Negro—The "school" of Slavery—Extravagant tribute of the Republican party to the beneficence of Slavery—The Negro obtained his *maximum* of civilization as a slave—Temper of the Southern people on Negro suffrage—The theatrical machinery of "the League"—Solidity of the Negro organizations in the South—The elections of 1867 in Virginia—A war of races imminent—The prayer of the South for peace—Interesting statement of Ex-Governor Perry of South Carolina—The feeling of *desperation* in the South—Danger of another and *peculiar* rebellion there—The recent farce of Restoration—The lesson of Fenianism—A warning, and not a threat, to the North.

The black thread of the Negro has been spun throughout the scheme of Reconstruction. A design is betrayed to give to him the political control of the South; not so much as a benefit to him, not so much out of solicitude for him—for a solicitude so large and disproportionate would be curious—as to secure power to the Republican party in the North, and to open new issues for it, since what was supposed to be its capital stock in controversy—the Slavery of the South—has been extinguished in a conflict of arms.

There is a distinction, running through the Anti-Slavery party, which has not generally been recognized, and which claims here a particular notice. The party contains two distinct schools, which we may conveniently designate as Abolitionists and Negrophilists. We are aware that many of those who made the most violent war upon Slavery sympathized with the Negro under the general head of an oppressed human creature, not out of any peculiar regard for his colour, or for any supposed extravagant virtues in his African nature. They adopted the cause of the Negro from general motives of humanity; they desired to free him; they desired to do for him such kindly offices as they would do for any suffering people; but they pretended to no special solicitude for the black man, because he was a black man, nothing beyond a natural sympathy for the cause of the oppressed. The candour of this portion of the Anti-Slavery party we may, and do respect; there was a large generosity in it—Quixotic it may be—but such as hunts the world for all instances of oppression, and for all possible occasions of virtuous controversy.

On the other hand, we find in the Anti-Slavery party a positive and most offensive disease—manifesting for the Negro a singular affection, devising peculiar rewards and gratifications for him, and intent upon making him the political pet and idol of America. We find this curious mania not only in white men of mean and scurrilous blood, but in some of the most cultivated ranks of Northern society—represented, for instance, by such men as Charles H. Sumner.* It is a diseased sym-

* The following reflection in a biographical sketch of Mr. Sumner contributed by the author to the periodical press adds something for the curiosity of the reader:—

"To look upon Mr. Sumner, as he sits in the Senate of the United States, in his Eng-

pathy, probably growing out of the excessive and impassioned contemplation of the Negro, as a victim of injustice. In some cases, it proceeds to the most offensive and abominable excesses; the black skin and the most unclean peculiarities of the Negro become objects of endearment; his African nature is endowed with romantic virtues; and the inevitable tendency of the mania is to an amalgamation of races.

These two parties—the Abolitionists and the Negrophilists—have strangely united in the present upon the Negro, as exhibited in the scheme of Reconstruction. The latter party needs no excuse for its zeal for the black man. The former would have, perhaps, been content with liberating the Negro, and showing him

lish cut of clothes and parliamentary shirt collars, and dainty linen, patting his mouth with scented handkerchiefs, or stroking his body with his large white, well-scrubbed hands, one would scarcely imagine him a victim of this loathsome disease. But strange as it may appear, there are instances of men of the most fastidious appearance and of extreme physical culture having morbid fancies for the Negro. The maudlin language about an 'infusion of warm tropical blood' into the cold Caucasian is not altogether that of the coarse ignorant natures of the North; and many of our readers will remember a Northern book on 'miscegenation,' in which this beastly suggestion was dished up with the garnish of a depraved philosophy, and horribly tricked out with tawdry flowers of rhetoric. We are aware that we dissect a delicate subject; but we must cut down to the tumour. We regard 'miscegenation' as an extremity of the disease of Negrophilism; yet an extremity more possible than is generally supposed even in minds apparently cultivated and natures apparently clean. To a fanatical philosophy like that of Mr. Sumner it may happen that nothing is unclean; and a long habit of regarding the most unsightly objects through the colours and prejudices of such a philosophy may even beautify them, and lead at last to an unnatural affection and embrace. Briefly, there is no appeal to old opinions or old tastes, when the disorder of 'Negrophilism' is once admitted into the mind; and there is no telling what transformations it may effect, or what riots of blood it may kindle in the depraved constitution of the fanatic. The distinctions between a moral mania on this subject and a positive physical disease, are alike difficult to define or to keep; and we insist upon the danger of an excessive regard for the Negro, no matter on what moral or sentimental grounds it may be first developed, running at last into physical affections of the grossest kind.

"We are very well informed that Mr. Sumner has an excessive regard for the Negro. We do not exactly know what are his opinions or practices on 'miscegenation' (which Mr. Wendell Phillips has already declared the hope and elixir of our future national life); we are not prepared to say what is the precise extent of his disease of Negrophilism; and yet the disease is so marked in him that we cannot well see where he can hold up the doctrine of equality short of the sexual commerce of races, and how, with his great solicitude for the African, he can deny him this bounty of the flesh."

an ordinary humanity; but they were confronted by the necessity of continuing themselves in power, and they saw in the Negro the instrument of their selfishness and ambition. It was thus the Negro was elevated into an importance exceeding all that he had ever claimed for himself, and new demands put into his mouth by the emissaries of party.

Never was delusion more foolish than that we had washed our hands of the Negro in the blood of the late war. The Republican party never entertained a thought of disbanding on the conclusion of the war. It found new occasions of controversy in Reconstruction. The development was: the political power accumulated and energized by the war continued in action, with the addition of a violent extreme wing, which always grows out of excessive party triumphs. The South did not see the interminable question behind Slavery, when it most ignorantly congratulated itself that the abolition of the latter had terminated dispute. The spectacle to-day is the Negro, who for more than two generations has been the pest of American politics, the conspicuous theme of legislation, the subject of new and larger contentions—a more important instrument than he has ever yet been in the hands of a radical and revolutionary party.

We are first struck by the inconsistencies involved by this party in their exhibition of the Negro in the Reconstruction scheme. Before the war, they were great sticklers for *homogeneousness*, North and South. "You cannot," said Mr. Seward, in his famous evangely of the "irrepressible conflict," "have one section free and the other slaveholding." Is it any more possible to have Negro supremacy in one section and white supremacy in the other?—is not the difference, indeed, more vast and conflicting, in proportion as the Negro is elevated into this new importance? The fact is the Republican party, in preparing another and an enlarged edition of the " irrepressible conflict," is drawing a yet deeper line of antagonism through the country.

The proposition of Negro suffrage, imposed violently upon the South, has been scouted by the North when applied to itself. Even the most radical members of Congress fly out against it, when it is to be imposed upon their own States and constituencies, and in the language of one of them (Mr. Spalding, of Ohio) declare that it "cuts directly across the Constitution." Another member of the Republican party in Congress (Mr. Lawrence, of Pennsylvania) adds the bold assertion that nine out of every ten Republicans in his district sustain the decision of Judge Agnew, that Negroes may be excluded from the company of white men in railroad cars and public conveyances. In fact, on no modern question of politics have the people of the North shown more sensitiveness than on that of entertaining the Negro as an equal at the polls.

In 1865, Negro suffrage was voted down in Connecticut, Colorado, Wisconsin, and Minnesota. April 6, 1867, a joint resolution was passed by the Legislature of Ohio to propose an amendment to the State Constitution, striking the word "white" from the franchise law of the State. A popular vote on this amendment was taken at the October election, when it was rejected by a majority of 50,269. In November, 1867, a special vote was taken in Minnesota and Kansas on proposed amendments to the State Constitution, extending the elective franchise to persons irrespective of colour. In both States, the amendments were rejected, by 1,248 majority in Minnesota and 9,071 majority in Kansas. In New Jersey, the issue was indirectly presented in the election of members of the Legislature, and the people returned a similar verdict; a majority of

16,354 against the proposition to enfranchise the Negro. The four States* which made such an exhibition of popular sentiment in the elections of last year, contained, according to the census of 1860, fully two millions of whites and about thirty thousand Negroes. If the Northern people could not permit this comparatively small number of Negroes within their borders to vote—if they could not risk the experiment of Negro suffrage to this very limited extent among themselves—on what principle of justice are we to account for the fact that so many of the Republican party insist that Negroes, supposed to be inferiour in capacity to the freed blacks in the North, should vote in States of the South, where they are nearly equal in numbers to the whites, and have, indeed, been made to exceed them by the frauds of registration!

In view of the figures above, we apprehend two facts: first, the hopelessness of imposing Negro suffrage on the North, and, second, granting it to be imposed, the little effect it would have on their politics and society, its incapability of qualifying the *irrepressible conflict* between Negro supremacy in the South and white supremacy in the North. Admit Negro suffrage in the North, and yet the supremacy of the white man is assured there—the most permanent principle in their society. The conflict is that of "enduring forces" between the reign of the white man in the North and the domination of the Negro in the South; the homogeneousness of the nation is gone; there is no longer a political identity in America; and a conflict, more vast and insuperable than any of the past, has taken place in our history. The Negro is no longer a topic of division between the two sections as a slave, but as a master and ruler,

* We may add the State of Michigan in 1868—rejecting Negro suffrage, although it gave the Republican ticket a majority of over twenty-nine thousand in 1866

asserting his political individuality, impressing society with his laws, and exhibiting his peculiar nature in acts of authority.

In view of this terrible sacrifice of the homogeneousness and identity of the nation, we have only this oft repeated argument of the Radicals: that there is a peculiar reason for endowing the Negro in the South with the suffrage; that it is necessary for his protection. We deny this necessity. The Negro may be protected without the ballot fully as well as other political minors in the community—unnaturalized foreigners, women, and persons not arrived at the age of twenty-one, all of whom have their civil rights, without possessing the elective franchise. But even admit the necessity of protection, concede to the Radicals all they have ever asked out of their peculiar tenderness for the Negro, and yet we are prepared to say, it is a small consideration, an utterly inferiour consideration, in view of that vast conflict which it must cause in our political system, a hiatus in our civilization, a surrender of the great interests of American progress to solicitude for an inferiour race!

And here we must surprise the reader by a quotation from one of the most remarkable of our living politicians. The extract is from a speech of the notorious Benjamin F. Butler, delivered in Salem, Massachusetts, shortly after the John Brown raid, and intended to re-assure the South. It is strange, indeed, to find this man of all others, supplying to the South the thought of the infinite inferiourity of the Negro by the side of the interests of the white man. The declarations he made, in 1860, are so applicable to questions now in Congress, and contain such a clear and admirable doctrine for the South in her present situation, that the reader is likely to pause upon them with curious reflections.

"The mistake is, we look at the South *through the medium of the Abolitionists—a very distorted picture.* *** These questions" [those of freeing and enfranchising the Negro] "which to us, locally, are of so little practical consequence as hardly to call our attention, are *to them the very foundations of society—ominous of rapine, murder and all the horrours of civil war.* And because the discussions of the question about Negro emancipation do not disquiet us here, we should be blind indeed not to see *the wide difference of such discussions to them,* if the results are reduced to practice.*** We have the right to form our own domestic institutions, as we please, to our own liking, and not to any other community's liking, and will exercise that right, and under the Constitution must be protected in that right. Every other State has the same right, to please herself in her own institutions, and *is not obliged to please us in her selection of them*; and as in duty, and of right bound to do, we will protect her in that right, whether we like them or not.*** *Human progress is not to be set back a thousand years, because of the difference of opinion as to the supposed rights and interests of a few Negroes.* As well might the peasant expect the Almighty to stay the thunder-storm which by its beneficent action clears the atmosphere of a nation from pestilence, lest the lightning bolt should in its flash kill his cow."

We have not exhibited this passage from the political life of Butler as mere proof of the inconsistency of the man, astounding as it is. No additions are needed to his infamy. We have quoted it in a higher interest; for the truth it contains, for its real intellectual merit. We are not prepared, indeed, to go to the length of the brutality which likens solicitude for the Negro to care for a beast of the field. But we do recognize the plain, general truth that the interest of the Negro is inferiour to that of the white man, and that our civilization and progress are not to be interrupted and surrendered on concessions to him.

It has remained for the Chicago Platform to suggest yet another argument, or semblance of argument, for Negro

Suffrage, *as in the South,* and to make a somewhat novel version of this article of the Radical creed, as will appear from the following language:—

"The guaranty by Congress of equal suffrage to all loyal men at the South was demanded by every consideration of public safety, of gratitude, and of justice, and must be maintained; while the question of suffrage in all the loyal States properly belongs to the people of those States."

The idea of Negro Suffrage as *a punishment* of the South logically admits that it is an odious and unnatural condition. But apart from this consideration, to fasten a measure on one section of the Union, for whatever motive, and to lift it from the other section, not only creates, as we have seen, a social chasm, but is of that inequality of laws, which is the prime condition of despotism, and is utterly inconsistent with republican government. It is the inequality, rather than the severity of laws, that constitutes despotism. The most severe laws have been tolerated, and have existed in republican forms of government, as long as they have borne equally upon the community, and have been fairly distributed over the surface of society; but, no matter what the law, or what its merits in the abstract, the moment it operates unequally, burdens one portion of the community and exempts the other, it becomes a hateful edict and a despotic oppression. This is the first lesson of constitutional liberty.

No party in the government at Washington, even if the subject of suffrage is fully admitted to be within its jurisdiction, has the right to propose one measure of it for the South, even as a penalty of rebellion, and another measure of it for the North, even as a reward for loyalty. We state the proposition as the Radical party itself has put it, in the very best terms, admitting its pretensions on every member of the argument, to show most conclusively its essential absurdity. But does not the antithesis of the proposition read more truly in the words with which Thurlow Weed, an eminent Republican, has paraphrased it:—"to declare that in one part of the country, where coloured suffrage is likely to prove ruinous, it may be established and enforced by superiour power; while in another, where such suffrage would be too inconsiderable to be noticed, it may be left to the people who have declared against it!" This is the true ground of distinction in the proposition, as between North and South; but even without reference to it, rejecting everything *ad captandum*, the division of so large a measure of legislation, the inequality of a law at the very basis of political society, would be essentially despotic, inevitably disorganizing, strange to every tradition of the country, and utterly inadmissable in "a government of the people."

Those who ask the ballot for the Negro sink at every step in the argument. It involves a price too great, even if he needed it; but we have argued that it was not necessary for his safety or preservation; and now we advance to yet another argument: that so far from the ballot being a benefit to him, it would involve him in a competition with the white man, eventually ruinous to himself, and be a direct invitation to what he has most to fear—a war of races. Let him beware of the poisoned gift. The ballot precipitates the war of races, to avoid which should be the highest effort of American statesmanship. It is the declaration of war between the Negro and the white man.

There is an instinct of humanity, a great unwritten law of nations, that one race only ought to have political power in the same country, each race in its own. It is a law that leads to internal peace, and to the national development and prosperity which that peace insures. The Negro has shown himself sensible of it, and wherever he has had power as a race, he has been unwilling to share it with the white man—as in Spain, in San Domingo, and in Liberia. In the latter country the white man is excluded by legislation from all political offices. It is the result of a natural law. For centuries the Negro has been known in both hemispheres as the enemy of the white man; and it is remarkable that he has never lived in friendship with him except as a slave. From Slavery he has derived all his civilization and benevolence.

The so-called Slavery of the South is properly defined as the school of the Negro. Declaim, as men may of the vices and horrours of that institution, we yet have the unanswerable fact that it carried the Negro to a higher civilization than any other agency ever applied to him; and the Republican or Radical party in claiming for him, that he is already qualified for the suffrage, implies a higher tribute to Slavery than its most zealous advocates ever urged—for it is Slavery that has educated the Negro to the point where the Republicans claim he is fit to vote and act equally with the white citizen—Slavery, which has thus returned him from its bonds an intelligent creature, fit at once for all the functions and trusts of the citizen! It is curious in what inconsistency the Republican party involves itself, when in one breath of declamation, as that of the rhetorical Mr. Bingham of Ohio, it describes the abolition of Slavery as "taking off the chains that have bound down the higher faculties of the Negro for more than two hundred years," and in another mood describes the same event as exhibiting the black man so improved by his experience as a slave from his original pagan and savage condition, as to claim by his intelligence and virtue all the privileges and immunities of the white man.

But we do not go as far as this extraordinary tribute of the Radicals to the beneficence of Slavery. It is extravagant beyond all that Southern men ever claimed for it. Holding that Slavery was a valuable school for the Negro, that by acting on his peculiar and strong imitative capacities, it gave him a certain reflected civilization, we yet do not believe that that civilization comes up to anything like the point of equality with the white man, and we are convinced that its *maximum* was obtained in the condition of subjection to the white race. Slavery has improved and civilized the Negro to a certain extent, and has now left him the subject of a new experiment. We would make that experiment kindly and tenderly, although we think it vain, as we believe the Negro obtains his highest development in the convenient position of a subordinate where he copies and imitates. This being the natural law of his inferiourity, we certainly would not force upon him the destructive and deadly experiment of thrusting him into a violent equality with the white man and substituting for the old and useful instincts of Slavery the principles of competition and rivalry. The Negro improved by copying the white man; Slavery made these copies convenient; but he will surely die, when the copy is broken, and competition becomes the new experiment. It is the law of nature, and no human legislation can change or obstruct it.

It is then this experiment of the equality of races, which must ultimately sacrifice the Negro; which offends nature's laws, and thus provokes a sure penalty; which shuts up ten millions of white people in the valley of humiliation and death; which wrenches all the laws and traditions of the country to a foreign and violent purpose; which legislates outside the Constitution; which engulphs the landmarks of our history and proclaims the most terrible and hideous revolution of modern times, that the Radical party of Congress has prescribed as the indispensable condition of the reconstruction of the South and the restoration of the Union. The policy is put before our eyes; the black cloud is hung up in the heavens; the prophetic signs draw nigh. In the North, the question of Negro reconstruction, except so far as it carries with it pieces of the Constitution and thus involves some ultimate questions of popular liberty, may be a dull and distant speculation. But the South is daily crucified upon it. Capital and enterprise are banished by the political commotion; men cultivate their fields as if they tilled the crust of a volcano, anxious only for the one year's crop; there is a daily terrour in every house; there is starvation in the pale faces of women and children; and in the eyes of desperate men there is a gleam like a flash of swords.

The population of the South is peculiar. Be it remembered that it contains tens of thousands of men, who have been baptized in blood, trained in war; who have stood on the burning edge of battle with their lives in their hands, and have feared nothing. They are a ready-made army. They are the men who count some things worse than the terrours of Death; more terrible the dumb sufferings of those they love than the loud agonies of battle; more terrible the wail of little children crying for bread than the blast of destruction in their ears. Their homes are ruined; their fields are black and sterile; their vines are withered; and life has but little for them. There are lengths of suffering and of insult which these men will not endure. Better death than the dregs of life; better convulsions than the

Stygean calm of despair; better the hiss and the storm of the red-winged battle than the dumb torment, the voiceless crucifixion of the soul.

The condition of the South is far different from what it was in 1865; and a war of races, then treated only as a distant speculation of scholars, has become an imminent danger to all practical men. At the close of the war the relations between the whites and the Negroes were kindly and amicable; there was a general disposition to co-operate in repairing the prosperity of the country and re-building on the ruins of the war. But this happy condition has been changed; and chiefly through the operation of those political organizations of the Negro masses in the South, effected by emissaries and agents from the North in preparation for the State Conventions and the Presidential programme of 1868. "The League" has introduced a new theatrical machinery in the politics of the South, the power of which on the peculiarly strong imagination of the Negro is almost incredible. It is like the influence of religious superstition on his African nature; its commands are superiour to all other calls and necessities; he will stop from work "in the middle of the row" to attend its meetings; he will slink away from his employer, after all protestations to the contrary, to vote the Radical ticket, at the secret command of this new political society, which, indeed, entirely possesses and governs him. No one can understand this peculiar condition of the Negro population who has not recently visited the South. Intelligent people in Virginia were utterly surprised at the solid array in which the Negroes lately moved to the polls in the vote for the Convention. They understand it better now, since the black hand of the League has become visible in the work.

Since the election there have been counted in Virginia eight hundred societies of the Negro, bound by oaths and holding secret meetings. From these conclaves there issued a solid organization of blacks at the memorable election of last year, as completely under the control of their leaders as an army under its General in time of war; not only marching to the polls to vote down conservative intelligence, but to vote down all moderate men, even those known as the prominent Union men of the State. Many persons of the latter class were hunted down, pelted with stones; the very few Negroes who attempted to vote the conservative ticket were threatened with death; and the police were assaulted when they attempted to protect the conservative blacks from the violence of men of their own colour. These scenes of furious brutality, and the evidence that ran through them all of a powerful, permanent organization, likely to repeat them at any time, have already impressed thoughtful men in the South with the idea that a condition, so monstrous, cannot be maintained, and that the attempt of reprisal or correction is inevitable.

It is in view of the solidity of these Negro organizations that Alexander H. Stephens, one of the tamest of Southern politicians and the least subject to alarm, has recently declared in Washington, with the utmost seriousness, that a war of races is imminent, and absolutely unavoidable if the Radical programme be prosecuted to extremity. If the New Orleans riot was repeated to-day, it probably could not be confined as it was in 1866, but might inflame the whole South. One blow struck now, and thousands of armed men may spring from the ground, and unutterable scenes of horrour ensue. It is this danger that disturbs the whole South; it is the daily peril of the volcano on which the home stands; it is the constant strain upon the imagination—for who can tell when Destruction may lift its red torch in the troubled air, and proclaim the conflict.

It is remarkable that the worst element of disorder in the South attaches to the uncertainty of the future relations between the Negroes and the Whites. We see industry palsied in all its branches from doubt of the security of its fruits; the most productive fields in the world lie uncultivated, and are shunned by capital; the great staples, cotton,* rice, sugar and tobacco, are no longer produced in those quantities which formerly made the South a commercial empire; the potential wealth of those States, which once nerved the arm of industry, and enriched commerce throughout the country, is lost to the nation. The future is observed through disfiguring mists of uncertainty; and the immediate prospect of restoration to the Union, under the Reconstruction laws, is only as Africanized States. From these scenes of present ruin and desolation comes the unheeded prayer for peace—that peace which was

* The efforts of England to build up her cotton culture have found unexpected assistance in the political radicalism of America. In 1861, the supply of cotton derived by England from the United States was seven out of eleven thousand millions of cwts., or seven-elevenths, while last year, out of a whole supply of eleven millions four hundred thousand cwts., the United States furnished four million cwts., or four-elevenths merely. The Reconstruction scheme of Congress operates as effectually as the war itself to stimulate and encourage the efforts which England is making in the cotton culture, and those efforts, through railroads in India, to which the British government gives liberal aid, are of an imposing character. India, where labour can be had for five cents a day, is penetrated by railroads thousands of miles in length, and lines of steamers communicate weekly with the Indian ports. The East Indies are now said to have more miles of railroad in operation than Spain, Italy, Austria or Russia, and nearly half as much as France. It is not deemed impossible that, when the home product of England shall be deemed adequate to her supply, she may even impose conditions upon the import of American cotton. Such are the lamentable results to our interests and pride as the greatest cotton-producing country of the world, which have followed the disorganizing policy of Congress, and which will be rendered still more ruinous by the success of the schemes now in progress for the transfer of the whole political power of the South to the hands of the blacks.

promised the people of the South as the fruit of their suffering, and the reward of their surrender in the war. The prayer comes to Congress in the most touching expressions. A late petition from the people of Alabama declares the willingness of the people to continue under military rule, rather than accept restoration on the frightful condition of Negro domination, and pathetically entreats Congress by appeals to a common race, a common civilization, a common Christianity, to save them from their tormentors. An address of the white citizens of South Carolina similarly invokes the justice and humanity of their race. They beg peace—nothing more than peace to enable them to build on waste places " our temples of worship, our sacred and ruined cities now lying in ashes, our dismantled dwellings and our prostrate credit, for its holy Christian influence, and for the civilization and refinement which spring up in its path." And these noble and pathetic prayers are unheeded by Congress, or burlesqued by a brutal wit, while the insolent demand of the Negro, grown to a threat, is treated with reverent regard and affectionate solicitude!

As evidence of the present condition of the South we have an authority even more temperate and judicious than Alexander H. Stephens. We refer to Ex-Governor Perry, of South Carolina—a gentleman who was inclined to the cause of the Union throughout the war, and who has obtained the respect of all parties for the candour of his opinions. Some of the results of his personal observation in the South are so coincident with the views we have already expressed, that we may adopt them in our narration. He describes the Negro as "no longer that industrious, useful and civil labourer which he once was, but an idle drone and pest to society. Inflated with his new and marvelous political importance, he has abandoned his former industrious habits, and spends his time in attending public meetings and loyal-league gatherings by day and by night. The whole race seem disposed to quit their work and resort to the towns and villages, where they may eke out an idle and wretched existence in pilfering and begging." The depreciation of real-estate, consequent mainly on the disorganization of labour, Mr. Perry calculates at one-half or two-thirds during the past year. Property at forced sales brings the most absurd trifles. He cites the instance of a plantation, well-improved, containing two thousand acres in Harry district, sold at public auction to the highest bidder for five dollars! No one wants land when there is no labour to put upon it. "A great many persons," says Mr. Perry, "are moving from the lower country, where there are so many Negroes, and that section of South Carolina is destined to become a wilderness. The same thing must occur in many portions of Mississippi and other States. A gentleman, just returned from Mississippi, testifies that lands which rented, in 1866, for fourteen dollars per acre were now offered at two dollars per acre, and no one would take them." The condition of affairs is summed in the following language: "our fields and plantations are uncultivated, the country pauperized, at the point of starvation and filled with every grade of crime." After describing the condition and temper of the South in different details, Mr. Perry concludes: "The present military force will have to be kept up to maintain peace between the two races, and there is no certainty of their ability to do this long. I have for some time thought that when the Negro government went into operation, it would be impossible to preserve the peace of the country. A war of races must ensue."

We have sufficiently traced some of the most unhappy elements of disorder in the South to the demoralization of the Negro. We pass to another point in the same field of observation. There is another danger than that of a war of races.

If we regard the lessons of history, the condition of the South is one of real alarm; because the people there are evidently verging to *desperation*, and this condition of mind is precisely that in which the worst and fiercest commotions take place. True, the South is incapable of a large and organized contest of arms; she has not the material or apparatus for another war, and her spirit is, in a measure, constrained by her poverty of resources. But it is not improbable that her patience may break at last, and that she may take that wild and desperate recourse to arms, in which a people maddened under despotism have even sought vengeance, where they could not accomplish relief. So far her patience has been exemplary; with the cessation of the war there was a cessation of all smaller essays of violence, almost unparalleled in history; and those who had supposed that the great contest could only terminate with a dissipation into the adventures and outrages of guerillas, were agreeably surprised at the solid and perfect peace which ensued almost immediately on Lee's surrender. For nearly three years thereafter the South has kept a peace more profound than perhaps ever followed upon a war of such extent and violence. Her people have hitherto been patient even under the worst excesses of Radical rule, because they have been fed with hopes and amused with prospects from one political season to another. But there is now apparent danger that the Radical party may experiment on that patience too long. They may plant too many thorns in the path of "reconstruction." The people of the South have waited upon the political "problem" at Washington only to find it become more and more involved and painful; we already hear the mutter of desperation; and before her white population is driven into the fatal angle of Negro supremacy, the last corner of their extremity, there is fear the ground will be marked with the blood of a desperate and indiscriminate conflict.

It is proper that we should understand here that certain recent proceedings of Congress, ostensibly admitting representatives from Southern States, so far from having advanced Reconstruction a single logical breadth, have really turned back the problem to its first premises and have accomplished nothing more than an ostentatious farce. Some thoughtless minds have leaped to the congratulation that certain Southern States have at last been re-admitted into the Union, when the fact is that they are still excluded, in every true and logical sense, from the equal benefits of the Union, and exist only as nondescript appendages of territory under permanent disabilities, insulted by the farce in which they have been marshaled as States restored to their political rights. Indeed, the prospect of restoration appears further off than ever, and the problem of Reconstruction becomes more confused and unmanageable, as new laws thicken around it.

When some months ago Alabama* applied for admission into the Union, the proceedings of Congress were tantamount to a confession, that it was intellectually incompetent to deal with the problem of the restoration of the South. In this case the whole matter of Reconstruction was remitted to a "provisional government," returned, indeed, to that policy which was so violently and summarily condemned in the President. The alternative was to exclude Alabama or to require her to relinquish her sovereignty, on coming into the Union. The difficulty in the mind of Mr. Thaddeus Stevens, which he freely confessed in

* The papers in the case of Alabama showed that only about 6,000 whites voted on the new constitution.

the course of debate, was not that the Constitution which this State tendered had not been adopted by the majority of registered votes, but that it might afterwards be changed, and that, therefore, a condition should be attached to the act of admission, to the effect that the people of Alabama should not make what laws they like, but only what Congress dictated—a singular mode, truly, of guaranteeing a "republican form of government"!

It has, indeed, been in such delay and entanglement of Reconstruction; such broken promises; such "confusion worse confounded," that the South has found her patience nearly expended, her hopes tantalized, and her resolution, no longer confined within the bounds of prudence, vaguely wandering to meditations of violence.

The issue was again presented to Congress by the application of Arkansas, and the condition, indicated by Mr. Stevens, was renewed to the effect that she should part with her sovereignty—that she should give an irrevocable pledge, never to change or diminish the concession of unlimited and unqualified Negro suffrage. In the case of five other Southern States (North Carolina, South Carolina, Louisiana, Georgia and Alabama—the last making a second application for the admission of her representatives) this pledge has ultimately been exacted by the House of Representatives, with some other conditions, in the following verbose form—

"That the Constitutions of said States shall never be amended or changed so as to discriminate in favour of or against any citizen, or class of citizens, of the United States, in their right to vote, who are now entitled to vote by said Constitutions respectively, except as a punishment for such crimes as are now felonies at common law, whereof they shall have been duly convicted; and no person shall ever be held to service or labour as a punishment for crime in said

States, except by public officers charged with the custody of convicts by the laws thereof; and that so much of the seventeenth section of the fifth article of the Constitution of the State of Georgia, as gives authority to Legislatures or Courts to repudiate debts contracted prior to the 1st day of June, 1865, and similar provisions in all the other of the Constitutions mentioned in this bill, shall be null and void as against all men who were loyal during the whole time of the rebellion, and who during that time supported the Union, and they shall have the same rights in the courts and elsewhere as if no rebellion had ever existed."

The bill from which we have quoted was carried through the House almost without debate; without effort to procure information as to the nature of these Constitutions, the vote upon them in detail, or their practical workings with reference to the ordinary interests of the communities upon which they were enforced. In many of these Constitutions, apart from the topic of the Negro, were singular excrescences of legislation; and to all of them attached a story of fraud and corruption. A Southern correspondent, treating of these reconstructed Constitutions says: "In South Carolina, Alabama, and Arkansas, the Legislature can keep up standing armies in time of peace, and in North and South Carolina, and Arkansas, children, irrespective of colour, are to be compelled to go to the public schools together, unless privately educated by their parents. In the Mississippi Convention, now [May 15, 1868] in the 127th day of its session, at a cost of a quarter of a million dollars already, there are but five white native Mississippians out of the whole one hundred delegates. In South Carolina, there are sixty-five Negroes in the House and nine in the Senate, and these ignorant creatures, who outnumber the whites on joint ballot, only pay $187 25 taxes, though their majority gives them full power of taxing all the property of the State. Fifty-seven of these Negroes pay no tax at all, and of the seventy white members thirty-six pay no taxes either, and the balance of them only $368 80; so that the whole South Carolina Legislature only pay $496 65 of the taxes it is to impose."

This budget of curiosities comes in the vehicle of the press. There was no disposition of the Radical party in Congress to ventilate them, or to give any information on a subject on which they proceeded to pass important and historical legislation. Nor was there any explanation afforded even of the condition proposed by Mr. Stevens, invading the relief sections of these Constitutions in reference to debts contracted during the war, and curiously giving pecuniary premiums to Union men. Even this remarkable novelty was passed almost without debate; and all efforts to criticise a body of legislation, so large and various, were peremptorily suppressed.

But it is not of this haste of legislation that we design to complain in this place, or of the customary suppression by an unscrupulous party of all statements of the means by which it obtains its ends. We have referred particularly to this pretended restoration of States to the Union as an insult to the intelligence of the South, and a new provocation to its patience. It is but a farce; a prolongation of the real problem of Reconstruction, which can never be completed, until the Southern States are re-admitted on the terms only of the Constitution, taking their equal and accustomed places in the Union. The intelligence of the South so far from being pleased with these recent proceedings of Congress, described in the extract of legislation we have just quoted, resents them as a deception and snare. Even the New-York *Times*, an organ, in many respects, of the Radical party in Congress, is forced to confess that it has yet done nothing to justly determine the essential questions of Reconstruction. This journal says: "Has the fundamental condition of the Arkansas bill been wisely determined as a precedent to be followed in admitting other States? Universal suffrage has been made the corner-stone of Reconstruction, but should it be so engrafted upon ten States that their own people shall be deprived of the power to introduce modifications? We say nothing now as to the difficulties inseparable from attempts to render partisan dogmas irreversible. We might ask, how a tradition of the Medes and Persians can become vital in self-governing communities, and how Congress proposes to enforce the condition, if the reconstructed States choose hereafter to disregard it. Viewed from a critical stand-point, the whole subject is so beset with difficulties, constitutional and logical, that we doubt the ability of any man to see his way clearly to the end of the road on which the country has entered."

Reconstruction, in its just constitutional sense is still far off; it will probably never be accomplished by the present party in power; the whole ground of legislation will have to be traversed again; and the serious question is whether the South may not be hurried to violence, as persecution presses, and relief hangs in the distance.

If that violence does ensue, there will be no question of prudent trials of war, no calculation of armies and material. The South is incapable of the grand *duello* of the past, but not incapable of the fierce and desultory rebellion of movable columns and raids; incapable of a war of calculation, but not incapable of a war of vengeance. She may repeat on a much larger scale the Fenianism of Ireland, and may even take a lesson from the few Indian tribes which have sufficed to hold a year's campaign against the military power of the United States.

Such vengeful rebellions, spread over the whole space of a country, renewing themselves rather from desperation than hope, and animated by the willingness of a people to die rather than suffer longer, have sometimes, as we are assured by history, been more difficult to quell than regular wars, and have shaken to their foundations governments stronger than that at Washington. Admitted that the South must ultimately go under in such a contest. What of that! There are times when men find their lives intolerable, and will wear them on their sleeves in any tilt at fortune. Let Congress beware of too much experiment on the temper of the South, for a rebellion may yet be kindled there, in which many men will be satisfied to find a funeral pyre, provided it consumes with themselves the structure of a hated and intolerable despotism. .... But we are not advising the South.—We are simply warning the North. We have stated what is the desperation of the former; but against that desperation we set our faces, and we write in these pages to counsel the true hope of the South. If we have represented an extreme case, it is that the rebound of the argument may be more striking and effective. There *is* hope for the South. Our mind has steadily held it in all we have written up to this point. From the condition we have described, of ruin and terrour, we shall presently see emerge Hope, pure and beautiful—like the white star, *alba stella*, rising after the storms of the day have been spent, and the torn and purple clouds have been gathered at the gates of Evening!

What is the true hope of the South?—The new cause, or the "lost cause" revived—Abolition destroyed the barrier of races, the true value of Slavery—The war, as merely developing the ultimate issue of constitutional liberty and of our political traditions—"The South Victorious"—The lesson of patience—Pessimists in Congress—B. F. Butler and Thaddeus Stevens—Can the Constitution be recovered?—Survey of our departure from it—Peculiar conditions for judging American history—An incident of the Philadelphia Convention—The elections of 1867—Power of public opinion in our political system—"White," the winning word—Declaration of Gen. Ewing—Congress translates the political controversy into a war for liberty—Two parties left by the war—The fundamental idea of President Johnson's Administration—Review of it—Horace Greeley and a New Jersey correspondent—Character of President Johnson—His extraordinary sacrifices of power and patronage—His heroic attitude in Impeachment—A bold and thrilling avowal—Value of his example to the South—The nobility of Hope.

What is that hope of the South, to which we have referred? It is the hope of a new political conflict, in which the South will stand stronger than she ever did before; in which she will find occasion to repeat what were really the most important issues of the war; in which she will have the opportunity to regain her "lost cause." She may have to endure much before she reaches the threshold and fruition of this new controversy; but the conclusion is sure to her. This new cause—or rather the true question of the war revived—is the supremacy of the white race and along with it and strengthening it, the re-assertion of our political traditions, and the protection of our ancient fabrics of government. This was the ultimate, logical problem of the war, although the people of the South but dimly perceived it. They were the wise men in the South who understood at the beginning, that Slavery was a most unimportant object in the war as a matter of property; that the abolition of Slavery was not to be greatly regretted as such—a small, incomplete event—but it was to be deplored as an introduction to the terrible and greater question of Negro equality, and such political reconstruction as we see attempted to day. They saw far ahead, who defended the condition of Slavery and counted it in the war, and throughout its term of existence as the barrier to the further and vaster question of races in America. It was in Slavery as this barrier, that the South had its most intelligent and valuable interest; and now, when this barrier is broken down, there must be a certain regret for that—a loss in itself considerable—yet a recognition that the greater contest yet remains, and that the higher cause of the political supremacy of the white man is *not* lost. Slavery was an outwork of the controversy; but the great battle is yet to be fought. The war has eviscerated and enlightened the true question, and the South prepares to contest it with advantages she never had before. When she defended Slavery by her arms, she was single-handed, and encountered the antipathies of the whole world; now, when she asserts the ultimate supremacy of the white man, she has not lost her cause, but merely developed its higher significance, and in the new contest she stands, with a firm political alliance in the North, with the binding instincts of race in her favour, and with the sympathies of all generous and enlightened humanity drawn upon her. Who will say, looking at the situation from this eminence of true philosophy, that there are not some subjects of congratulation and hope for the suffering South? It is this true hope which the author would proclaim; summoning the South to the appealed and sublime trial of a cause, diminished it may be in respect of some subordinate questions, but not lost in the logical and vital issue. It is a new summons, a new inspiration; the sound of the trumpets is beneath our windows, and the blood in our veins sings as we go forth to the last and proudest contest of American liberty.

"The South victorious" may yet be the ultimate conclusion, as Wendell Phillips spoke the words at the close of the war. But it will be the victory of the white man; the victory of the Constitution; the victory of law and of tradition—a victory crowned with noblest fruits and flowers—and may God speedily grant it!

But the people of the South must learn this sublime lesson of life: that often the grandest achievements, the most glorious of human endeavours and triumphs must commence in a term of suffering; that patience is the preliminary period of the greatest deeds, the condition that foreruns the most perfect successes. He who learns to wait, says a French proverb, is master of his fortune. The South must wait and suffer, before she can realize the true hope we have declared for her. She must wear the crown of thorns before she can assume that of victory. She must endure much from Congress; new insults, perhaps fresh devices of torture; treading the wine-press, traversing a dreary and crooked routine; but the end comes at last, and with it the assured triumph and reward.

The precepts of religion and the doctrines of philosophy have united in the formula of Patience; and history illustrates its conquests in the lives of nations as well as in the individual examples of virtue. It is the jewel of Christianity. It is the ornament of a true manhood. It is the title to all great and permanent success; and he has imperfectly apprehended the meaning of life, who does not see its relations to human achievements, to the restoration of man to whatever he has forfeited or lost. It is at once the consolation and lesson in all afflictions, in all trials, from the time when man first worked out his spiritual redemption to that in which he regains any lost cause of virtue and truth.

"He in whose hands all times and seasons meet,
What if He hath decreed that I shall first
Be tried in humble state and things adverse,
By tribulations, injuries, insults,
Contempts, and scorns, and snares, and violence,
Suffering, abstaining, quietly expecting,
Without distrust or doubt, that He may know
What I can suffer, how obey? Who best
Can suffer, best can do.—"

Paradise Regained.

There are men in Congress—false and malicious prophets—who would persuade the South that there is no hope for her, and that she might as well succumb to the fate they have prepared for her. They scoff the idea of any modification of their terms, and they already show a determination, not only to disregard, but to defy whatever of change has already been apparent in the popular sentiment of the North. Have the last year's elections, those great Democratic triumphs in the North, been of any real, practical advantage to the South? They have not been followed by any softening of the Reconstruction policy; on the contrary, Congress hardens and exaggerates its programme; and we see after these elections the unification of military rule in the South, the dictatorship of Grant, the outrage of Stanton, the wound to the Supreme Court, a fresh list of exactions and usurpations. The South, says Butler—that muddy bilious monster of the bloated face and the crooked eyes—speaking to the Virginia Convention, should not hope for better terms; for whatever other changes may take place, the Radical majority will be maintained in the Senate for six years to come. Then gets up Thaddeus Stevens, in his unclean old age, to expectorate, that the people of the South are vagabonds and nondescripts "outside the Constitution," and that, so far from being assured of the end of their sufferings, the list of penalties should be prolonged with "mild confiscation," and whatever else the ingenuity of their "conquerors" may suggest.

There is a hideous significance about this old man, preparing in the last moments of his own life new instruments of torture for the South, and grinning over the work of his bony and unsightly hands, at the very side of his own grave. It is an exhibition of what hate and passions legislate for the South—a picture of diabolism at which the heart shudders.

But we are not to be too much impressed by the weak and wicked declarations of such men. True, Congress may be competent, during its official term of insolent power, to deal with all the questions of Reconstruction, and the South may have that stock of iniquity to endure, that path of thorns to tread; but the people speaks at last, and although to retrace whatever steps may have been taken, may be difficult, it will not be impossible. The political slate will be wiped clean at last of the scrawl and filth; and as the people, in our system of government, can never surrender its conscience to any permanent form of legislation, the work of reform is never impossible.

We are not seriously disturbed by the rhetorical bravuras of Ben. Butler, or the acerb expectorations of Thaddeus Stevens. It will not be long before such men descend to the grave, or expire in the pillory of public contempt. Their expressions are the splutter of malice. But apart from their excess, we recognize a serious question, exciting the thoughtful anxieties of men least disposed to take alarm, or to be moved by the threats of mere personal animosity.

We are painfully aware, that some of the most intelligent minds in the country have already entertained a question of the possibility of the restoration of the Constitution, and of the recovery of the liberties it was designed to secure. They doubt whether this can be ever accomplished by human means, or otherwise than through some providential event recalling the nation to its better senses, and giving it the opportunity to disembarrass itself of party and to re-adjust and settle the Constitution in the spirit of a true patriotism. They argue that the Republican party has already progressed too far in power to be recalled; that they have already destroyed the integrity and independence of the Executive Department; that they are steadily encroaching upon the Supreme Court; that they have already broken up the fundamental and vital distribution of political powers in the Constitution; that at each stage of this progress to despotism, they have disdained the challenges of popular sentiment; and that in view of this insolent career of usurpation, public interest has been so tame and impassive, that it is unlikely to make any serious obstruction to the now not distant consummation of the revolutionary design.

It is time to notice how far we have wandered from our former political courses, and where the tides of controversy have carried us. In the commencement of that great speech of Daniel Webster, in 1830, which arrested the progress of Disunion, the orator and statesman said: "When the mariner has been tossed for many days in thick weather, and on an unknown sea, he naturally avails himself of the first pause in the storm, the earliest glance of the sun, to take his latitude, and ascertain how far the elements have driven him from his true course. Let us imitate this prudence, and before we float farther on the waves of this debate, refer to the point from which we departed, that we may at least be able to conjecture where we now are."

The departure from the law of the Constitution, the original standards of our political system, is, indeed, vast and alarming on the retrospect. It has taken place by stages so numerous and so ingeniously calculated, that the public mind has not been sensible of the distance accomplished; and now, on looking back upon it in a single and inclusive view, the impression is that of painful surprise. The whole structure of the Government is changed. The President is no longer President, and Congress claims nearly every power formerly exercised by him. By the tenure-of-office law, it has really divided the Executive of the nation into seven or eight different Presidents, independent of, and superiour to the one elected by the people, whom he can neither control nor remove. Each Secretary is President over the whole sphere of his Department, having the power, to the exclusion of the President elected under the Constitution, to order the army, to control the national funds, to manage foreign relations, to regulate the postal service, to administer the affairs of the internal revenue. Each of these seven or eight Presidents, again, is controlled by a branch of Congress, and has no other limit to his authority, and no other rule of responsibility. A right is taken from the President elected by the people, without which he cannot perform the duty expressly commanded of him, to take "care that the laws be faithfully executed," or fulfill the obligation of his official oath, to "preserve, protect, and defend the Constitution of the United States." Other usurpations have taken place. Congress has almost practically destroyed the Executive office, and, at the same time, has erected absolute military despotism in ten of the States of the Union. It has done this in destruction of every authority reserved to the States by the Constitution, as well as every individual right of life, liberty, and property, reserved in the same way to their people. It is quite clear that if these usurpations receive for much longer time the approval of the people, the hope of the recovery of the Constitution is gone, and ultimately with it the prospect of individual freedom, and the vital idea of our institutions.

We state the argument in its full force. Unhappily, too, the attempt at despotism in America has taken the form and direction of Legislative usurpations; a form the most dangerous to liberty, and the most difficult of opposition. We recognize the force of this peculiar fact; and we are reminded of the declaration of Chatham, when, choosing between the arbitrary power of the Crown and that of a House of Commons, that "tyranny in no shape is so *formidable*, as when it is assumed and exercised by such a number of tyrants." It is obvious in our system of government that the very worst depository of unlimited power would be a large legislative assembly, like Congress; where the very number diminishes the responsibility of individual members, and enlarges the influence of popular passions. We recognize then the peculiarly powerful form which the revolutionary tendency in our country has assumed; and we recognize, too, that other dangerous element in the situation:—the comparative impassiveness with which the people have viewed the usurpations of Congress, and its advance to the eminence of despotic power.

Yet we do not despair of the republic. It was to be expected that the popular sensibilities with respect to liberty should be greatly blunted by the late war; it was one of the worst effects of the war; and the diminution since of the concern of the people in the conduct of their government is painfully apparent. But that concern has not entirely ceased;

and the peculiar intelligence of the American people is sure to reproduce it. It is with respect to this intelligence and the native generosity of Americans, that we claim some exception from the precedents of history. In America there are unusual conditions. The extraordinary intelligence of the people enables them to recover quickly from errours and surprises; and their love of liberty is so traditional that it is not likely to be seriously affected by any temporary causes. It is remarkable that in no circumstances does an invocation to liberty, even in the merest platitude of a Fourth-of-July speech, ever fail to awake in the American heart a generous emotion, or to obtain some response from the multitude.

An incident in the Philadelphia Convention, summoned to consider the state of the country, in 1866, gives proof, so shortly after the war, that the spirit of '76 was not entirely extinguished in the American heart. The Convention adopted an address which was read from the clerk's desk. It referred to the usurpations already commenced by Congress, to reduce the Southern States to the condition of conquered provinces; and in this connection it was declared: "The ten millions of Americans in the South would be unworthy citizens of a free country, unfit ever to become guardians of the rights and liberties bequeathed to us by the founders of this republic, if they accept with uncomplaining submissiveness the humiliations thus sought to be imposed upon them!" The preceding argumentative points of the address had been listened to with quiet and deliberate attention; but when the words, just quoted, were pronounced, there was a universal acclamation of the Convention and its audience; men rose to their feet to cheer the sentiment, and for a time the voice of the speaker was lost in the volume of applause. The loud shout that went forth from the hall was a signal and a testimony to the country.

It was a happy augury. Its promises have not been realized, as rapidly as we could wish; yet there are evidences of progress, and occasions of encouragement. The elections of the last year in the Pacific, East, West and Middle States, show an awakening of the people—a disposition to recall from the Republican party all of that exceptional support which was given it during the war for the specific purpose of saving the Union. The people demand the fruits of the war; and the same motives that committed them to a party, especially sworn to save the integrity of our institutions, now operate to recall the trust, and to punish its abuse. Within one year, nearly a quarter of a million votes have been gained by the Democratic party and measure the change of public sentiment.* This is the significant exhibit of

* In a recent speech Senator Doolittle exhibited the following table of votes to show the comparative strength of the conservative and radical parties in 1866 and 1867. It includes all the States represented in Congress, except those which held no election in 1867. The table is as follows :—

States.	1867.		1866.	
	Dem. and Con.	*Rad.*	*Dem. and Con.*	*Rad.*
California	49,995	42,447	26,245	33,221
*Connecticut	47,575	46,585	43,433	43,974
Iowa	58,880	90,798	56,483	90,926
Kansas	19,421	10,443	8,151	19,370
Kentucky	103,392	33,939	95,979	58,035
Maine	45,644	57,462	41,947	69,637
Maryland	63 739	22,110	40,264	27,351
Massachusetts	70,360	98,306	25,671	91,980
Michigan	55,865	80,819	67,708	96,746
Minnesota	32 663	35,809	15,755	35,137
New Hampshire	32,663	35,809	30,481	35.137
New Jersey	67,468	51,114	64,336	67,525
New York	373,029	335,099	352,526	366,315
Ohio	240,622	243,605	213,606	256,302
Pennsylvania	267,751	266,824	290,096	307,274
Rhode Island	5,340	7,554	2,816	8,197
Vermont	11,510	31,694	11,292	34,117
West Virginia	13,393	14,694	14,943	20,573
Wisconsin	68,873	73,637	55,414	79,318
Total	1,628,183	1,578,748	1,457,146	1,741,135

* In the elections in Connecticut, April, 1868, the whole number of votes cast was 97,761. Of which the Democratic candidate for Governor received 49,666; and the Republican candidate 48,095—a Democratic majority of 1,571.

the elections of 1867. If the voice of these elections has not been so commanding as to create a pause in the despotic and reckless course of Congress, it at least assures that it will soon summon to power those who will execute its will.

Our political system is singularly impressible by popular sentiment; it has no permanent depositories of power; it admits no life tenures of political office; it is emphatically a government of public opinion. The peculiarity of popular revolutions, especially in America, is that the reactionary forces carry the people further in opposite direction than those which previously impelled them. When the reaction does occur from the boundary of Radicalism, we may expect that it will go over a wide ground and to a point even of extreme virtue.

The idea of Butler that an accidental Radical majority in the Senate, for six years to come, can stand against whatever contrary influences there may be in all other departments of the Government, and in all other organs of public opinion, is as preposterous as it is insolent. There are limits to human effrontery; limits where even the vilest and most audacious men cease to brave public opinion, and sink in their own shame. In the case proposed by Butler, the Senate could not for a week survive the storm of public opinion.

"There are times," says an eloquent Senator, "when public opinion is like a placid stream gently flowing within its banks, when slight obstacles may for a time arrest, or change, or divert its course. Then it may be said, the voice of the people is the voice of the politicians; the voice of the people is the will of a party. But there are other times when the heavens are overcast, the rains have descended, and the floods have come, that its majestic current rolls on, emblem of wrath and power, when resistance maddens its fury and increases its strength.

Then it overflows its banks. The barriers of party caucusses and politicians are all swept away, and become mere flood-wood on the surface of the troubled waters. The voice of the people is no longer then the voice of politicians; then it is that the voice of the people is the voice of God."

Let us come back to the true hope of the South. It is to enter bravely with new allies and new auspices the contest for the supremacy of the white man, and with it the preservation of the dearest political traditions of our country. "WHITE" is the winning word, says a North Carolina paper, and left us never be done repeating it. The very word moves the instincts of the voting population of the North; it is the irresistible sympathy of races, which will not, cannot fail, when it comes to the last hug of the conflict, and perhaps blood spots the arena. It is this instinct which the South will at last summon to her aid, when her extremity demands it.

We admire a recent exhibition of courage on the part of South Carolina, a manly and hopeful protest which she has sent up to Washington against the Constitution enforced upon her in the farce of restoration. "You may make us pass," say the protestants, "under the yoke and we shall have to do so, but by every means which God and Congress have left us under the Constitution and laws, we will resist this domination of an inferiour race by peaceful means, by political efforts, by industrial agencies. We will carry on this political contest until we regain the control which of right belongs to the power of mind and the influence of virtue." These words are as sensible as they are noble; they contain the best and bravest spirit of the South.

The appeal of the South to the natural affections of race is one that essentially transcends all considerations of mere political party. It is an appeal reserved for the last extremity; the power of which may not be developed, when the question is merely speculative, but which essentially and instantly developes itself, when the issue becomes practical, and the contest grows to one of force. The public has lately had an assurance from a distinguished military officer, that, however the army of the United States may be attached to General Grant, and obedient to the orders of the political party in power, it would never serve as an ally of the Negro in a war of races. "I earnestly wish," writes Gen. Thomas Ewing, "to be in accord with the great party of my Kansas and army friends, and still hope to unite with them in supporting General Grant for President. But I want first to know whether he approves the Reconstruction measures; for if he does, I cannot support him. I regard them as mischievous—begot of revenge, misdirected philanthropy and lust of power. * * * Such a government cannot long have the heartfelt sympathy of any large body of white men anywhere. Blood is thicker than water, and Northern whites will sympathize with Southern whites in their struggle to shake off the incubus of Negro rule. If there were no prejudice of race to affect their action, the Northern people would still refuse to reproduce in the States of the Union, Hayti or San Domingo, * or any other government and civilization the Negro race has established since the flood."

* The allusion to the story of San Domingo is such a worn commonplace in recent American speeches that the public appears, from the very triteness of the reference, to have lost distinct recollections of the event. Few know this terrible history, so commonly referred to. A glance at it in the pages of a single writer (Bryant Edwards) is not out of place here.

"To detail," says the author, "the various conflicts, skirmishes, massacres, and scenes of slaughter which this exterminating war produced, were to offer a disgusting and frightful picture—a combination of horrours wherein we should behold cruelties unexampled in the annals of mankind; human blood poured forth in torrents; the earth blackened with ashes, and the air tainted with pestilence. It was computed that within two months after the revolt first began, upward of two thousand white persons, of all

Meantime, while the affection of race has not yet been fully summoned in the contest, the great point of advantage with the South is that the Radical party has necessarily identified its scheme of Negro supremacy with revolutionary designs upon the Constitution, and that the contest is thus broadly translated into a war of liberty. To enforce its scheme of Reconstruction, Congress has found it necessary to break through the restraints of the Constitution; to bind and gag the South with military rule; to besot the conscience of the Government; to buy the souls of men; to drug Grant; to close its doors alike to the interference of Executive authority or that of public opinion; to erect itself into a revolutionary body. The issue is thus widened, and the question of the Negro acquires all the significance of a second rebellion;—for, as President Johnson says: "To attack and attempt the disruption of the Government by armed combinations and military force is no more dangerous to

conditions and ages, had been massacred; that one hundred and eighty sugar plantations and about nine hundred coffee, cotton and indigo settlements had been destroyed (the buildings thereon being consumed by fire), and one thousand two hundred Christian families reduced from opulence to such a state of misery as to depend altogether for their clothing and sustenance on public and private charity! Of the insurgents it was reckoned that upwards of ten thousand had perished by the sword or by famine, and some hundreds by the hands of the executioner!"

On one occasion, we are told, the standard of the insurgents was "*the body of a white infant which they had recently impaled on a stake.* * * "A poor man, named Robert, a carpenter by trade, endeavouring to conceal himself from the notice of the rebels, was discovered in his hiding-place. The savages declared he should die in the way of his occupation. Accordingly they bound him between two boards, and *deliberately sawed him asunder!* * * *

"All the white and even the mulatto children whose fathers had not joined in the revolt were murdered without exception, frequently before the eyes or clinging to the bosoms of their mothers." * * *

"In the neighbourhood of *Jeremie* a body of mulattoes attacked the house of Mons. Lejourne and secured the persons both of him and his wife. This unfortunate woman—my hand trembles while I write—was far advanced in pregnancy. The monsters, whose prisoner she was, having first murdered her husband in her presence, *ripped her up alive and threw the infant to the hogs. They then (how shall I relate it?) sewed up the head of the murdered husband in——! !* Such are thy triumphs, philanthropy! And such an act was committed by mulattoes, some of whom had received an education in France! What may have been the deeds of the untaught Negroes!"

the life of the nation than an attempt to revolutionize and undermine it by a disregard and destruction of the safeguards, thrown around the liberties of the people in the Constitution."

This is the true breadth of the question—and the South will do well to seize and hold it, for here on this ground will be the dominant line and crest of the battle, here the point of victory. It is the august cause of the Constitution; and it is the good fortune of the South to represent in this high and important contest not only the conservative, but the traditional party of the country. It is the party which stands on the defensive, making its stronghold in the ancient fabrics of the Government, uplifting the banner of the Constitution, appealing to all there is of veneration for the past, reviving the lessons of ancestral wisdom—those of Jefferson and Madison—and putting these grand and powerful appeals against a faction, whose whole purpose is to interpret the past war as a political revolution, and to make it the era of departure from the tried and established standards of the past.

We come to ask: what is the true, historical significance of the past war? And in the light of this question, we perceive but two great parties: one contending that the war decided only the certain special questions for which it was invoked, and that the country is re-committed to the Constitution as formerly, and must be recalled to the condition and law of the past; the other violently construing the war as a pervading revolution in the body politic, trying to establish upon it a vital change of polity, and prone to all the new and rash experiments of reformers. It is hardly necessary to say which of these two parties is logically the stronger, and more likely to triumph in the end. The power of the first is its appeal to the past, the engagement of all the emotions summed in the word "patriotism." The true hope of the South, the excellent fortune of the South is, that in her peculiar contest for the recovery of her liberties, and her protection against the revengeful and revolutionary design that would dedicate her to the Negro, she not only appeals to the instincts of race, but she embraces the great monuments of law and tradition in the country, clinging to them—these sacred altars of safety—under the banner of the Constitution, and beneath the pointed shields of the fathers of the republic. Under this banner she is happily ranged in the contest; here is her strength, and hope, and animation, and assurance of victory; *in hoc signo vinces.*

The political contest at Washington is at last resolved into a re-assertion of the Constitution, on one side, and an open and revolutionary defiance on the other, an experiment of disorder and rebellion. It is in this sense that President Johnson has acted, rather than in any lower sense of fealty to the Democratic party, or peculiar affection for the South. We must acquit him of both these charges, when we find him in every conjuncture, and at every point of contact with Congress, proclaiming the virtue of the Constitution, and disdaining every lower argument or appeal. The sum of his administration so far is: an anxious desire to restore the country to the condition of the Constitution, to terminate the war at the boundary of the Constitution; hence his policy for an early restoration of the Union, with a provisional government the only stepping-stone to it—hence his opposition to all extra-constitutional terms imposed upon the South, to Negro suffrage, to probationary periods of military law, to all artifices of delay—hence his vetoes of the legislation of Congress to make an impossible problem of Reconstruction, and to involve with it an even greater element of discord than that which the late war extinguished. This is the extent of his offence to Congress—this the extent of those high titles of fame he will hold in history, when the judgments of mere party are humbled and forgotten.

But it is said the President has no jurisdiction, no constitutional care of the subject of Reconstruction; that his recommendations of policy thereon have been in derogation of the rights and conscience of Congress. Now, whatever may be said in a technical point of view, it must be remembered that the President as the constitutional head of the nation has the right to advise and recommend on all subjects; that in our political system he is the source of all enlightenment and advice.*

* We notice that General Grant, in accepting the Radical nomination for President, assumes a certain virtue in promising that, in case of his election, he will have *no policy* of his own, but will obey "the will of the people" etc. It is perhaps the least happy of the political brevities of a man not much given to words. As President of the United States he can only know "the will of the people" through Congress, and in obeying that body he becomes the servile representative of the dominant faction of Radicalism, taking all of his policy from the propaganda of such men as Stevens, Butler, Bingham, etc. But if he did not mean this, if he meant nothing practical, and only designed a demagogical phrase, then the platitude is puerile and shallow enough to be characteristic of a mind quite as much at loss for ideas as for words. "The will of the people" is the catch-phrase of a poor intellect, and Grant has, no doubt, had recourse to the political copy-book for an easy moral sentence.

Practically, the words cannot be taken as less than a servile subscription to the Radical majority in Congress. But even independent of party sense, they contain a theory of the President's office, so mean, that we fervently hope the utterer will never be permitted to disgrace it. General Grant is mistaken in supposing that the office of the President of the United States is mechanically to execute the laws, and that it is a virtue to have no policy of his own. Here he has fallen into the errour of a low mind, and has shown an utter want of appreciation of the dignity of the Presidential office. If his theory were correct, then any stick might answer for President; and it would be impossible to explain how an officer, who can originate nothing, who is incapable of any "policy" of his own, who was simply to register the edicts and perform the bidding of other branches of the Government, could yet be esteemed the first in honour and dignity, and stand at the head of the nation.

The infelicitous speech of Grant gives occasion for a commentary on the true nature of the Presidential office, confused as it has been by recent events. The President of the United States is vastly more than an executor of the laws, and it is both legitimate and proper for him to have a "policy" on all public questions. In our political system the President is the fountain of advice, the source of all political enlightenment; in his recommendations to Congress he is capable of advising and instructing on all subjects; he is looked to by the nation for universal moral counsel. This is the true and lofty interpretation of the President's office; and to say that he shall have no "policy" on cer-

By the way, an anxious correspondent in New Jersey has recently put this neat and novel question to Mr. Greeley of the New York *Tribune*: If Congress has excluded the representation of the South in its body, how is it that it assumes to legislate for it on the subject of Reconstruction—representation being the only and sole source and condition of Congressional authority; or in the very words of the correspondent: "If the President be President of the whole country, the Supreme Court the Supreme Court for the whole country, and Congress, Congress only for the States represented, is it not evident that the whole business of Reconstruction is entirely out of the

tain subjects, because Congress alone has the right to legislate upon them, is to belittle his great office into a servile acquiescence, and to make it a matter of no account who may dwell in the White House. We are aware that it has become recently fashionable thus to speak of the President as a cypher; it is part, indeed, of an attempt to erect Congress into a despotic tribunal; and it has become critically important that we should re-adjust our notions of the President's true position in the Government and restore it to its traditional importance. The most eager contests in our political history have been as to who shall be President; the nation has looked on him as its head, and the world has derived opinions of particular periods of our history from the character and conduct of the men who have for the time filled what was considered the first office in the gift of their countrymen. The President is thus something more than an "Executive Chair," a mechanical contrivance to carry out the laws; he is the prime political counselor of the nation, dispensing his advice periodically through the country; and to be without a "policy" in these circumstances would be simply to ignore his office and to neglect his duties.

We want a President with a policy—an abundant policy—penetrating every concern of the country, embracing all its cares, ready to be questioned and challenged by every interest in the land. This is our idea of a President: a man ready to advise the country in all respects, giving tone to its mind on all subjects, in sympathy with all its forms of intelligence; not a creature of two words, skulking behind non-committals, insisting that he has "no policy," which means in fact that he has no ideas. Save us from this inane creature, shuffling his platitudes and catch-words about "the will of the people," and insisting that there are no other elements to be considered than the pleasure of Congress, or the breath of the multitude. The science of government is a large and intricate one: there are other things beside "the will of the people"—laws, institutions, precedents, traditions, intelligence. We might pardon General Grant's "no-policy" speech as a piece of wretched tyroism in politics, the fault of ignorance, but for the meanness of the sentiment, his willingness to degrade an office honoured by the most illustrious memories in America to the position of an instrument of the Radical party in Congress. If he hopes to purchase the office by advertising his willingness to degrade it, he has miscalculated the sentiment of the people, and the respect they have always insisted on bestowing upon the first office in their gift.

province of Congress, and belongs exclusively to the President and the Supreme Court?" This New Jersey correspondent is evidently anxious, and a sincere inquirer after the truth. He implores Mr. Greeley not to "beat around the bush," but to "answer squarely and honestly," as then he will "hit the right nail fairly on the head for thousands."

The New Jersey correspondent has made a neat and unanswerable argument. Mr. Greeley is unable to reply to it; so he tries the *reductio ad absurdum*, and declares the doctrine of his correspondent a short cut to Secession and Revolution. Suppose, he says, the little State of Delaware was to refuse to send representatives to Congress, then by the correspondent's logic, she might nullify the acts of Congress, defy the revenue laws, land free goods to be distributed far and wide, and bankrupt the Government, while disintegrating and collapsing the Union. This is the reply of Mr. Greeley. But it contains a fallacy as plain as a pike-staff—letting alone the figure of the correspondent about the nail and hammer. In the case supposed by Mr. Greeley, Delaware would be unrepresented by her own wrong; to be sure, she must take the consequences of her own wicked election. But the ten Southern States are unrepresented, not by their own wrong; they have sent representatives to Congress; they have besieged its halls by all sorts of application and argument for their admission; and when Congress, by its own act, and deliberately, excludes them, and denies representation to these States, it debars the right to legislate for them, it cuts off "the sole source and condition of Congressional authority." Mr. Greeley cannot answer the question of his correspondent; it is novel, incisive, and goes to the very heart of the controversy.

A few words are appropriate here of the spirit which President Johnson has displayed in his collisions with Congress; for we are persuaded it is precisely this spirit that should be communicated to the South—that contains whatever there is of hope for her, and points the path to victory.

He has been patient, self-continent, profuse in sacrifice, and firm and sovereign in his trust of the ultimate result. There is one trait in the character of Mr. Johnson which has never failed of the admiration of the Southern people, in any shape or style of man, and which, even in the heats and resentments of the late war, obtained respect for him from the most violent Secessionists. It is his high, personal courage. No politician in the country has a more abundant record of this virtue. The man who on the threshold of the war could face the combination formed against him in the Senate by the most violent representatives of the South there, making him their especial target, converging their weapons upon him and say in front of the audacious array: " these two eyes never looked upon any being in the shape of mortal man that this heart of mine feared;" the man who, in 1861, confronted a mob at a railroad station in Virginia and, by a gleam of high courage in his face, overawed and disarmed them; the man who, when the Confederate armies overran Tennessee, and the Federal General Buell was thought to exhibit signs of despair, could declare in the capital of that State: " any one who talks of surrendering I will shoot; " the man who has firmly and conscientiously exercised the high office of President against the clamours and threats of a faction, sworn to take his official life, murder him politically and cast his flesh to the black images of their idolatry, must, indeed, have a firm and mettlesome spirit —possesses, indeed, that bravery of soul which is at once the auxiliary and ornament of the highest virtues.

Let this, too, be observed to his honour. The course of his administration has been to abdicate power and patronage; to chastise personal ambition; to overcome temptations, greater than ever assailed any predecessor in his office. Had he chosen the part of a Cromwell or a Napoleon, a servile legislative assembly would have been at hand to prompt and sustain him in the character of usurper and to constitute him the greatest military despot of modern times. Had he acquiesced in the scheme of Reconstruction prepared by Congress, he would have secured its bad alliance, and, through his office as commander in-chief, have found himself absolute master of the lives and fortunes of ten millions of people residing in the military districts of the South. It was the spectacle of a legislative assembly, in order to gratify its political passions, not only offering the executive chief despotic powers, but prompting him to their assumption and eager for his acceptance. Congress laid at his feet the absolute empire of nearly one half of the country, a patronage the most enormous in history; and had he accepted them, he might well have defied the feeble discontent of the South, while Congress would have been complaisant and he would have blazed in the encomiums of the most numerous party in the North. What then constrained this man, thus tempted—the temptation safe, the temptation even calculated on a balance of popularity for the acceptance—to deny and spurn it, to mortify his ambition, to reject the counsels of the most numerous, to sacrifice power and popularity together—what but the high, severe overruling sense of duty, which absolves from his selfishness, and makes him the sublime minister of the eternal laws of truth and justice.

The opposition of President Johnson to Congress never recoiled at the threat of Impeachment. Thus, although it had been possible for him to have been the idol of Congress, and to have soared on its adulation, the country has lately seen him standing in uncertainty and submission, an accused man at its bar! The sublime choice is all his own. We believe his brave heart in that noble utterance to the Senate of the United States, when the motion to impeach him was suspended over his head, and the sword had not yet descended: "If I had been fully advised when I removed Mr. Stanton, that in thus defending the trust committed to my care my own removal was sure to follow, *I would not have hesitated.*"

Looking back upon the administration of Mr. Johnson, we are struck with its evidences of self-negation. Yet, these denials are the price of true greatness, at once the discipline and the policy of the loftiest ambition. He has chosen the narrow path—that path which though beset with difficulties and hunted and hounded by persecutions, and planted with thorns, and lost in many parts to the world's observation, ascends at last from the black and poisonous shades and passes through fields of glory to the illuminated portals of History. Let the South emulate his course, his self-sacrificing policy, his brave patience, his enduring resolution. There is nothing like a single, high, personal example to animate and instruct a distressed and bewildered people; and fortunately the South has it in Andrew Johnson. There is no better, briefer lesson for the people of the South than that every man of them should practice this high example. Once this man, in a crisis, not greater than that of to-day, standing in the Senate of the United States before a close array of hostile faces said: "I have taken my position; and when the tug comes, when Greek shall meet Greek, and our rights are refused, after all honourable means shall have been exhausted, then it is that I will perish in the last breach; yes, in the language of the patriot Emmet, 'I will dispute every inch of ground; I will burn every blade of grass; and the last intrenchment of Freedom shall be my grave!' "

These are thrilling, memorable words. They suit the present contest of liberty; they are fit for the inspiration of the South. Let us repeat them and breathe our souls into them, and put them as fire into our hearts. No cause is ever lost for the true and noble; the soul of the brave man defies the accidents of fortune, and finds an ultimate inspiration in itself, though fate wreaks its worst upon his life, and tortures, and blackens it, and tears the very flesh from the immortal spirit. What man of the South will not repeat the words of Richelieu:

(*Richelieu*)—" Old—childless—friendless—broken;—all forsake—
All—all—but——"
(*Joseph*)—" What?"
(*Richelieu*)—" The indomitable heart
Of Armand Richelieu!"

Let us never despair. Hope is beautiful; it is grand; it is the property of noble souls, "the possession forever" of the destitute and desolate. Only the weak and mean surrender to despair. Come trouble in the life of the brave man—come falsehood and injustice and loss and scandal; come the finger of scorn and the arrow of misfortune; come all the multitude and baneful train of sorrows, and yet, yet he will hope. It is God's own law, which only the weakness and crime of humanity pervert. There are times when the heavens grow dark, and when wild, bitter winds wail in the great hollowness around us, and the heart of man sinks in contemplation of the scene; but to the patient the cloud will break at last, the glorious sun will ride into the golden gate, and the chambers of peace and beauty will again be hung up in the sky.

IMPEACHMENT.

The true revolutionary sense of the proceeding against the President—Its relations to Reconstruction—Errour of the Radical party—Growth of public interest in Impeachment—Anticipations of "the future historian"—Value of Impeachment as a moral exhibition.

We have already referred to the late Impeachment of the President as logically part of the Reconstruction scheme, the culmination of the effort to nullify the restraints of the Executive authority upon the will of Congress which designed to govern alone in the South, and to complete there an unqualified despotism. It is well known that the immediate question of Mr. Johnson's attempt to remove Secretary Stanton from the War Office was but the slight occasion of his arraignment, and that the real difficulty in the mind of the Radical party was, that the President was an impediment to their reckless and revolutionary policy.

It was fortunate, however, for the country that Impeachment was lodged on this particular issue and that personal resentments of the Radical party clouded their usual prudent judgment. In no part of the general scheme of the Radicals could an issue have been made with more disadvantage to them, or one better exhibiting the President to public sympathy, besides putting him on his strongest grounds. It was so complicated by additions of personal insult and outrage to the President; it contained so many elements, was such a combination of injustice, that we may congratulate the country that the Radical party, in its passion, fell into the errour of making a decisive question where the aggravation of circumstances was all against themselves, and where, so to speak, prejudices to their disfavour necessarily accumulated on the side issues. The question was thus multiplied in a remarkable sentence of a speech of Mr. Eldridge, Democrat from Wisconsin: "How is it possible for this Government of several co-equal departments to exist, when they are not only warring with each other, but when one keeps a spy, a common informer in the confidential councils of the other, and more than that a known and determined enemy, holding his position against his own professed convictions of constitutional right and duty!" *

*No better argument could have been devised for the President in the case of Impeachment—no more admirable vindication of his right to control the inferiour executive offices of his Administration than that contained in the speech of Mr. Thaddeus Stevens, before he had grown gray in the services of political iniquity. The extract is from a speech of this man, in 1837, on the question of amending the State Constitution of Pennsylvania, so as to deprive the Governor of powers similar to those lately wrested from the President of the United States. If Mr. Stevens had only repeated the same sentiments at the bar of the United States Senate, *mutatis mutandis*, he would have gone to the extreme lengths of the Democratic party, and have even outbid the arguments of the President's counsel. Such is the inconsistency of public men in our unhappy country, wno sacrifice all the truth and principle of earlier days to schemes of personal ambition and afterthoughts of party!

"Having reluctantly but inevitably come to the mournful conclusion, that all the vital parts of this venerable and hitherto venerated Constitution of ours are given over to immolation, as a sacrifice to the restless spirit of change which has taken possession of this Convention, I do not address you on this occasion with the hope of staying the hand of destruction which is raised against it; but simply to offer reasons which, to my mind, are all-powerful for resisting the depredations which are making upon this article of *the great charter of our rights.* * * Why take the appointment of the Heads of Departments, Surveyor General, Attorney General, Secretary of the Land Office, and Auditor General, from the Governor? *They are essentially a part of his Cabinet.* His own comfort, and the comfort of each of them, as well as the public interest, require that *there should be perfect harmony and unity of views and action among them.*

"But if you take the appointments from the Governor. it may, and probably often will happen, that he will be of one party, and entertain one set of principles, and they be of another party, and hold entirely opposite principles; discord and opposition must then disturb their counsels, and injure the interests of the State. * * * The Governor and

Here was a whole bundle of questions; and each multiple of the proposition was in favour of the President and the country, as against Congress. The latter, indeed, could not have tried a weaker link in the lengthened chain of "Reconstruction." It could not have made up a case more against itself; nor could the country have had a more favourable trial of its liberties, nor the South a better test of its hopes than in this proceeding against the President, in which the Radical party clearly admitted personal malice at the cost of political prudence. The country had a large, visible stake in the trial; the South had peculiar interests and hopes bound up in it; while what might have been the immediate personal consequences to the President was of comparatively little concern, even to himself, since we were well assured that he was equally able to endure martyrdom sublimely, as to bear victory gracefully, in behalf of patriotism, and in vindication of truth.

the Senate would either be of the same political party or hostile parties. If of the same party, the Senate would be no check upon the Governor, as there would be perfect concert before the nomination, and therefore this supervising power would be useless. *If they were of hostile parties, constant and bitter collisions would exist between them, which would greatly disturb the faithful discharge of their other duties.* * * * This work of ruin seems not to be exclusively confined to one party. True, all the members of the one party, whatever might have been their views when they came here, now act in perfect concert in stabbing the Constitution.

"They cunningly enough suppose, that if this amendment prevails, they can always secure the spoils of office, either through the Governor or the Senate, as they may always fairly calculate in having one of them in their favour. For, when the burdens heaped upon the people by that party become so heavy that they can no longer be borne, and their Governor is hurled from power, the Senate is not always also changed. *Thus patronage being their object, they act unitedly.* While many gentlemen of the other party, with an ostentatious magnanimity and a childish simplicity, either from the mistaken dictates of conscience, or to show their perfect independence and freedom from party trammels, join them in their headlong course. The struggle here, therefore, is a vain one. But I have full confidence in *a steady and disinterested people; disinterested as to the fate of parties, but deeply interested in the welfare of the State,* and the protection of the lives, the liberty, and the property of its citizens. Send forth to them this *mangled, mutilated, and deformed Constitution,* and they will put their seal of condemnation upon it; and they will still live and prosper under the well-tried charter which their wise and honest fathers left them."

Happily, these proceedings have terminated substantially in favour of the President, and the Radical party reels from the bar of the Senate with a wound reaching to its vitals. There is danger, however, that the country may value this success too highly; it is certainly not a triumph to be reposed upon; the wound to Radicalism is serious but not necessarily mortal; and it is only under a shower of blows that we can dispatch the monster. Something has been gained for constitutional liberty and for the "lost cause;" but it is rather new auspices and hopes than perfected results.

In looking back upon Impeachment we must admit that, for some time, there was a light and unbecoming display of public attention, with regard to an event unparalleled in American annals, that was one of the most serious and fearful signs of the times. The lesson of history is, that popular impassiveness is that condition in which Despotism easily accomplishes its purposes, and that levity is the frequent mood, the shallow and hideous mask, of the worst and cruelest revolutions. The question of Impeachment was so grossly misrepresented as one of mere personal consequences, that it was astonishing how such deception could be practiced even for the shortest time upon the boasted intelligence of our people. The true importance of the proceeding was revolutionary; it was the question of the integrity and independence of the Executive Department of the Government; the question whether we were to have a President, as in past times, or a cypher, without power even to regulate his political household; the question whether Congress was at once to ascend to the eminence of Despotism, and make the President of the United States its convenient creature, under the constant threat of impeachment,

"The hangman's whip, to keep the wretch in order."

As the trial of the President progressed, public opinion seems to have gradually risen to the level of its importance; and the spectacular curiosity at Washington was replaced by a serious interest, until at last the vote was taken on the most important article, on the 15th of May, at the height of one of the most memorable excitements in the history of our country.

We rejoice that the ultimate effect of Impeachment has been to betray the revolutionary design of Congress, and draw it from the ambuscade of false and hollow pretenses. These, indeed, have been fortunate and timely revelations. When the country saw Congress proceeding to the last extremity to destroy the independence of the Executive office, it was not likely on due reflection to ascribe so important a movement to any particular offenses of Mr. Johnson, especially since the Radical party constantly endeavoured to sink the question of his guilt or innocence in the proceedings; it perceived a permanent design, a distinct revolutionary purpose; and it at last appeared to be fully awakened to meet and to contest it. The Radical party logically became by Impeachment a revolutionary party; its act, in this particular, connected with the whole scheme of Reconstruction, was of a piece with military domination and Negro suffrage and other misgovernment; and the distinction of Impeachment, in the despotic series, was only that the outrage was conspicuous and aggravated.

The future historian who will write on the subject of the Impeachment of the President of the United States will be impressed by the novelty of the event, and will naturally find occasion in this *cause célèbre* to measure the morals of political life in America. He will notice its dramatic accessories, and produce a narrative varying between history and biography.

He will be struck by the popular impassiveness in which the Impeachment was commenced; but he will find that such impassiveness ensued from ignorance and misrepresentation. and will discover the increase of public interest until it mounted to the true importance of the event and apprehended its revolutionary significance. He will be surprised at the levity and insolence with which the President's accusers conducted these grave proceedings. He will notice the twitting debate in Congress, the jocose allusion, the amusement of the House when Butler drew the picture of Johnson returning to Tennessee at railroad speed, or when the bottled imp described the lofty argument, in which the President made his last appeal for the Constitution as "a plea of not guilty, with a stump speech in the belly."* But what will most excite his attention and employ his reflection will be the exhibition of moral depravity in our public life, which attempted to make a purely political speculation of the highest judicial proceeding known to our laws. He will curiously notice in all the abundant commentaries of the press, that the question of guilt or innocence was invariably subordinated to that of party expediency; that the votes of Senators were calculated with reference to the discipline of a party, or the prospect of a Presidential nomination, or some concern of patronage; in short, with reference to anything else than that issue of guilty or not guilty, which has generally been supposed to be the end of a judicial investigation. He will find that these vile calculations of the trial were made every day in the newspapers without exciting reproof or alarming the conscience of any one. In this single circumstance he will see the moral degradation to which public life in this country tends; and his pen will naturally pass to a broad commentary on the corruption of our politics which, commencing in the war, accumulated in the recess of Impeachment and threatened to stagnate in the chamber of the United States Senate.

Yet at the end there will be something to record of triumphant vindication of our people from these first reflections, of noble satisfaction in the disproof of those vile calculations of votes on the score of party policy. It will be seen that those calculations were, at least to some extent, disappointed; and indeed, in this moral display in our public life, the vote acquitting the President obtains an interest which vies with that of immediate political consequences. By this vote, a victory of law was proclaimed; a severe, if not a fatal wound, was given to a party that had heretofore been as insolent as it was injurious; an exhibition of moral integrity was made in one of the highest places in the land; and an event took place that for once adorned the history of our whole people.

But a story of disgrace yet lingers. There is a page in history that cannot be expunged, that will keep in infamous memory all the vile resorts of the Radical party, their appliances to procure conviction, their attempts to bring to bear upon men sitting in a judicial capacity the force of the organization, discipline, opinions and wishes of a political party. We give the mildest historical phrase to the interference of the Radical party, the recollections of which are so recent. It will rankle in the memory of Impeachment. All through the last week of the trial, the Radical journals teemed with efforts to use the force of asserted local opinions on the approaching judgment of the Senate; and it is notorious that a deliberate appeal, signed by the Radical Executive Committee, went from Washington to procure from all parts of the country the manifestoes of political party to affect the High Court in its brief period of advisement.

We have a peculiar satisfaction in the acquittal of the President, when we contemplate the amount of influence summoned from every extremity to procure a different result. This reflection not only confirms the triumph of justice, and gives additional pangs to the defeat of the Radicals, but it exhibits an amount of virtue, of moral integrity in the highest of public bodies known in America, that must be pleasing to our national pride, and conspicuously honourable in the eyes of the world. It is in this exalted interest that the vote in the Senate will be recorded in history. It is, indeed, an interest which no party can appropriate, which belongs to the entire community, and which will at once be recognized by all persons who have at heart the fame of the country, and consider the moral vindication that Impeachment has afforded even superiour to its justification of a political cause.

V.

DUTY OF THE WHOLE COUNTRY.

THE DEMOCRATIC PARTY.

Three duties of the country—Summary of the virtues of the Democratic party—Singular attempt of the Republican party, in 1861, to appropriate Democratic principles—Its return to Consolidation—Renewed appeal of the Democratic party to "time-honoured principles."

There are three points to be considered in that political regeneration which is the true hope of the South—three great duties of the country.

1. To return to the past, over the tract of the war, to re-assert the authority of the Constitution, to revive the political traditions of the country, to consult anew the fathers of the Republic, and draw from these ancestral lessons instruction and inspiration meet for the occasion.

2. To let the Negro severely alone, as a subject of political controversy, and, after properly providing for him in matters of civil rights, and doing for him the common offices of humanity, to leave him to gravitate to the condition which nature and experience shall assign him.

3. To organize into some party that shall override all sectional questions, that shall be coincident with the Constitution, and make no other test than fidelity to this instrument, developing the patriotism of the country within its limits and under its standards.

If any other party fulfills this condition better than the Democratic party, then let all patriots embrace it, whatever its name, and devote to it their names and services and fortunes. Here we have a party, brave and coherent; a remarkable party —remarkable, because it, alone, in the history of political opinions in this country, has maintained its organization since the foundations of the Government; because, it has ruled the country in long seasons of prosperity, and obtained the tests of experience and the inspirations of victory; because, it has administered the Government for much the better half of its existence; because, it is attended by the most glorious recollections in American history, and by the *éclat* of immortal names; because, in all times and circumstances, it has avowed the Constitution, and made it the paramount issue; because, recognizing in the vital articles of its own existence the principle of decentralization, it is constantly capable of an expansion limited only by the length and breadth of the American Union, and attending with equal steps the growth and progress of the country. It is this principle of decentralization, peculiar at once to the Democratic party, and to what may be called the political system of America, that manages and harmonizes the diversity of interests in our great Union; that secures individual rights; and that supports the inestimable doctrines of local independence and self-government. Of these doctrines an eloquent Democrat has written: "Without them the Union will be forever endangered. With them it will fulfill the hopes and prayers of all patriots. They furnish the key to unlock the magic chambers of our future. They are the safe and golden mean between the extremes of faction"—

> "The wisdom of a thousand years
> Is in them. * * * * * *
> Turning to scorn, with lips divine,
> The falsehood of extremes."

The Democratic is the only existing party in the country that boasts "time-honoured principles." Judged by the results it has accomplished—and there is no juster test—it has been one of the most beneficent parties in history. When Mr. Seward boasted, in 1860, that the Republican party was about to take control at Washington, Mr. Hammond, a distinguished Senator from South Carolina, replied that the Democratic party would surrender the country "without a stain upon her honour, boundless in her prosperity, incalculable in her strength, the wonder and admiration of the world." He described the achievements of that party, continuing his reply to Mr. Seward: "We have kept the government conservative to the great purposes of government. We have placed her and kept her upon the Constitution; and that has been the cause of your peace and prosperity. Time will show what you will make of her; but no time can ever diminish our glory or your responsibility."

That the Democratic party should have maintained not only its organization, but a distinct identity for so long a period and through so many changes in our experience as a nation; and that even it should have survived the mutations of the past war, is a remarkable phenomenon and testifies to an extraordinary virtue. The party appears to-day the only permanent thing in our political history; a firm link to the past in the multitude of changes that have befallen us. The tribute of Martin Van Buren in a posthumous work* is significant in this respect: "The long continued support of a majority of the people—the only test of political merit in a Republic—has secured a preference for its principles of which it may well be proud; and the general fidelity of its members to the faith they profess is creditably illustrated by the fact that after all the changes to which its organization has been exposed, its ranks, whatever may be the case as to some of its leaders, are mainly composed of men with like dispositions with those by whom that organization was effected." It is this identity of which the Democratic party is especially proud; tracing the descent of its principles from the fathers of the Republic, the same in defeat and in victory, and even emerging from the changing and deforming influences of the past war with undiminished similitude to what it was in earlier and better days of the country.

The patriotic contributions of the Democratic party in the past are historical, accomplished facts. However it may have wandered on particular inferiour questions and thereby lost power for a time, it is remarkable that the affections of the people have recalled it, on all occasions when the general principles of the Government are to be decided. Whenever the question has been between the Constitution and the limitations of authority in the general government, the Democratic party has won on its favourite doctrine of a distribution of political power. A most curious evidence of the strength of popular affection for this peculiar Democratic doctrine is the attempt of the Republican party to appropriate it, in 1861, and to incorporate it into the immediate creed on which they came into power. How the avowals of the latter party have been falsified,

* "History of Political Parties."

and they have reverted to the worst heresies of Consolidation, the world knows and the present day bears testimony. But that Mr. Lincoln and his party did, on their first concession to power, attempt to conciliate the people by upholding a Democratic model of government, so far as questions of political power were concerned, cannot be denied, in the face of the deliberate and official language of that occasion. In the platform upon which Mr. Lincoln was elected President, and which he repeated in his inaugural speech "the maintenance inviolate of the rights of the States, and especially of the right of each State to order and control its own domestic institutions, according to its own judgment exclusively, is essential to that balance of power on which the perfection and endurance of our political fabric depend." Again, before the hypocritical design of the Republican party had been accomplished, it was declared by Mr. Lincoln and his Attorney-General, Mr. Bates: "absolute, despotic power over the lives, the liberties, or the property of freemen, exists nowhere in a republic, not even in the largest majority of the people."

These assertions are interesting now. They attest the essential power of a principle belonging exclusively to the Democratic school, and they suggest how faithless and criminal has been the party that attempted to appropriate it for a temporary popularity. The time has come when, again, a general appeal is made against Consolidation, when all other political concerns are sunk in comparison; and we may expect the Democratic party again to march to victory on the supreme field of controversy. It is an appeal which, if made single and dissembarrassed, has never failed of success. It comes to us now with a peculiar force added by time and circumstances. If the American peoole believe, as they have frequently testified by their votes, that Consolidation leads to despotism, that to rule a territory so vast as theirs by a single free government, is impossible, we may expect that the appeal against the experiment has strengthened from developements of the past, and that the argument has increased with the growth and greatness of the country. It is an argument which prevailed when we had three millions of people. It is an argument which returns to us now, when our limits extend from ocean to ocean, and when our population is quite forty millions, with the prospect of being eighty to one hundred millions before the end of the century!

THE GROWTH AND GREATNESS OF AMERICA.

Curious prophecies of Adams and Jefferson—America in 1776—Retrospect of Mr. Jefferson's Government—Two pictures at Washington—Three visions of an empire in America—The Alleghanies, the Mississippi River and the Pacific Ocean—Summary of the present resources of the country—A lesson of the late war—Value of the physical greatness of America, as a source of patriotic inspiration—A new interpretation of the Union—The peculiar danger of a revolution against the Constitution—A remarkable fact about European Emigration—The problem of America, territorial consolidation (not political consolidation)—President Johnson's tribute to the Union.

Two of the most remarkable men in the early times of America were Thomas Jefferson and John Adams. Both of these illustrious statesmen who had commenced manhood in colonial times, who had been co-adjutors in the cause of the Revolution, who had occupied, in turn, the eminence of President of the United States, and who had carried into retirement the reputation of sages, rendering Quincy and Monticello twin names of the political oracles, had had remarkable visions of the future greatness of America. That of Mr. Adams was more wonderful, and accomplished a larger interval of time.

As early as 1755, the future statesman of Massachusetts, then only twenty years old, wrote to a friend from his meditations at Worcester: "Soon after the reformation, a few people came over into this new world for conscience sake. Perhaps this apparently trivial incident may transfer the great seat of empire into America. It looks likely to me; for, if we can remove the turbulent Gallics, our people, according to the exactest computations, will in another century become more numerous than England itself. Should this be the case, since we have, I may say, all the naval stores of the nation in our hands, it will be easy to obtain a mastery of the seas; and the united force of all Europe will not be able to subdue us!" It was a bold prophecy, even to repeat, when Mr. Adams saw the independence of America accomplished, and the new impetus of enterprise, and new career of progress dated from this great event.

At the Revolutionary period, America contained 230,000 white people, and was a ragged piece of territory between the seaboard and the mountain ranges, extending about a thousand miles on the Atlantic coast from the Penobscot to the Altamaha, and averaging a width of not more than a hundred miles. If one will take a pencil and trace on the map the course of the American settlements of that day, he will mark out a thin country, an irregular border upon the bays, harbours and inlets, averaging a hundred miles inland from the coast, with here and there a projection to the bases of the mountain ranges and even some slight tendrils winding through the fertile valleys of these natural barriers. Without steam, without canals and even without tolerable highways, the population of that day hugged the ocean, or clung to the banks of such rivers as furnished convenient means for transporting heavy products to or from the seaboard. In Virginia, the settlements were mainly in the river bottoms of the tide-water region. There were already some efforts at migration westward; but although they had penetrated the Alleghanies, and made some "clearings" in that part of Virginia which is now Kentucky, they were but juts in the geographical outline, and had scarcely more than blazed the pathways of adventure. The great Mississippi was unknown but as a distant landmark in the possessions of a foreign power; the valleys of the Illinois, Wabash, and the Ohio, were scarcely habitable for civilized men; the Atlantic slopes even were yet contested by Indian tribes, and Thomas Jefferson, the third President of the United States, had been born at Shadwell, a short distance from Monticello, when the trails of the hostile Monacans or Tuscaroras were yet fresh on his lands and through the adjacent hills.

Yet Mr. Jefferson counted ten millions of freemen under his authority as President; and people of those times, looking at their expansion and increase, began to think that the vision of Mr. Adams might be something more than the vagary of a self-constituted wise-acre. But Mr. Jefferson's government was a small affair compared with the statistical standards of the present; and it is curious to look back upon the anxieties of his day, and measure them with the mighty concerns of the present. Think of the annual expenditures of a government averaging only six hundred thousand dollars, and yet a clamour about economy; the entire standing army of the United States a single brigade, consisting of two regiments of infantry and one of artillery, and yet a jealousy of the military power; a public debt of fifty-four millions, twelve millions of which were only owed abroad, and yet its management an occasion of the greatest alarm, and Hamilton's "treasury schemes" denounced as the foundation of an overshadowing plutocratic power in the United States! Put against these the present annual expenditure, of which but a single item, that of the War Office, *and in time of peace, too*, is $177,000,000;* a military establishment numbering 56,000 men; and a public debt of $2,500,528,827, by the last monthly account of the treasury, May 1868,—and we may have some idea of the vast interval between the government of Jefferson and that of the present imperial concern at Washington. They are as far apart as two different ages—pictures as unlike as if they were brought in confront from the most distant quarters of the earth; and although our progress is, of course, not measured by these figures, which are to a large extent exceptional, yet they sufficiently indicate how our ideas have expanded when they can take into easy and undisturbed calculations such standards of magnitude, which, sixty years ago, would have been simply incredible.

The greatness of America seems to have first become a serious and practical thought with the great additions to its territory made by Mr. Jefferson. These, including the purchase of Louisiana and the treaties with the Kaskaskia Indians, the latter acquiring a broad belt of territory extending from the mouth of the Illinois River "to and up the Ohio," actually doubled the area of the United States, and opened startling visions of empire. Mr. Jefferson had a prophetic mind with reference to the Great Valley of the Mississippi, which was

* The expenses of the War Department for the month of March last are set down at $13,960,000—a greater sum than the whole yearly expenses of the Government under John Quincy Adams.

then almost *terra incognita* to his countrymen; he saw the vital necessity of the use and outlet of the great river, when he declared, "I would not give one inch of the waters of the Mississippi to any nation." The value of the acquisition may be estimated from the facts that this river is two thousand miles in extent, with one of its tributaries doubling the parent stream in its length; that it drains by its waters 1,200,000 square miles; that it floats the internal commerce of twelve States, and that the steamers thus employed were accounted, before the late war, to be worth sixty millions of dollars. It is to-day the vast interests contained in this river, which, more than any other natural cause, maintain the balance and integrity of the American Union; it has contributed to the homogeneousness and unity of the nation; formed its character and civilization; and put it in the precise position wherein to control forever and indisputably the destinies of the western hemisphere.

On the acquisition of the Mississippi River, Mr. Jefferson proposed: "When we shall be full on this side, we may lay off a range of States on the western bank, from the head to the mouth, and so, range after range, advancing compactly as we multiply." The advance of "range after range" has been made beyond his expectations, and the third vision of empire —the first bounded by the Alleghanies, the second embracing the Mississippi—now unrolls to the shore of the Pacific Ocean. Few persons, even of the present day, have comprehended the extent of this last and most effulgent apparition of the greatness of our country. A new territorial phrase has come into vogue, and we speak of "the Pacific slope" after the same idea in which we spoke sixty years ago of "the Atlantic slope." It is the new natural feature of our territorial empire. In a recent report of the Land Commissioner at Washington, "the Pacific slope" is described as 1,000 miles long and 680 miles wide, with an area of over 831,000 square miles, or about 5,000,000,000 of acres—sufficient to inhabit 100,000,000 people, that is, not only to give them room, but to afford, from its varied and bountiful resources, all the subsistence of civilized life. How much of this and our other vast Western possessions is as yet uninhabited, even to the extent of not being "claimed" by settlers, or appropriated to railroads, may be judged from the fact that there is yet the immense amount of 1,400,000,000 acres of public land, including the lately acquired Russian territory—a vast domain as yet unpartitioned to enterprise, unvexed by grants, with the title of the Government slumbering in it, awaiting the advance and solicitations of a civilization that has not yet approached it.

The total area of our country (not including Alaska) is calculated at 3,250,000 square miles—larger than the whole of Europe; exhibiting all the ranges of climate from St. Petersburg to Canton; and nearly one-third of this vast domain, that is one million square miles, is gold-producing, stretching from British Columbia to Mexico, containing two States and four territories, and yielding minerals reckoned, since 1862, at one hundred million dollars per annum.

It is thus not only the magnitude of spaces we have to deal with. Territorial expansion adds affluent fields of civilization and industry and opens almost interminable avenues of enterprise. The animating prospect on the Pacific slope is not limited by the ocean, but reaches to the producing regions of Eastern Asia. The trade of the Indies, of China, of Japan, of all the eastern world, must flow into this country, and throughout this country to the rest of mankind. We are already 3,000 miles ahead of England in our routes to China, Japan and the Indies; and an official assurance is given from Washington that, by October, 1869, the main Pacific Railroad will be finished, and the great steam horse will carry us from New York to San Francisco direct.

From the very base of the Rocky Mountains we have already the intelligence that this Railroad has been completed to that point, and that, five hundred miles from Omaha, the locomotive is still pushing its way westward. It is a great and marvelous fact—an exhibition of American vigour—almost without a parallel even in these progressive times. A few years ago Omaha itself was an unknown spot, in a trackless wild, almost unindicated in our geography; now five hundred miles west of it to Cheyenne City, at the base of the Rocky Mountains, we have a railroad completely equipped, aud so closely followed by population and industrial enterprise that its net earnings for one quarter of the past year have been nearly half a million dollars; this amount being realized from its local business. When the road is completed, it will form a single line of 1,830 miles, passing through Dakota, Utah and Nevada, with feeders running from Colorado and Idaho, and with connections again branching east from Omaha to Chicago, running down to Cincinnati and St. Louis, and terminating in the great Atlantic cities, New York, Philadelphia and Baltimore, accomplishing a distance of over 3,000 miles across the continent, and forming a great connecting link between Europe and Asia, opening to the Old World the shortest route to China and Japan. It is a mighty picture, a grand diorama of progress, a new age of commerce. For one thousand years the stream of Eastern trade and travel has flowed in one direction; now a new highway is designed for it, which wil' transport the commodities of Asia along with the treasures pouring in from the mines of our new Territories, and stock with homes and all the appliances of modern civilization a wild country, hitherto a haunt for savages, and a dismal curiosity in our geography

But one generation ago there was scarcely a railroad in America. Now we have 37,000 miles of completed railroad in this country, which, since their commencement, is at the rate of 1,000 miles a year; and there are in course of construction 17,880 miles of railroad. For many years after the revolution, manufactures was scarcely a recognized branch of American industry. By the returns of the last census they amounted in value to $1,900,000,000. The first decennial census estimated our annual exports at nineteen millions of dollars. The census of 1860 showed them as more than four hundred millions of dollars, whereof all but twenty-seven millions were of domestic production. Within the memory of the present generation Great Britain was undisputed mistress of the seas. In 1860 the United States had the largest fleet of merchant vessels afloat, Great Britain second, France third, and Germany fourth. In the same year the real and personal estate of our people was estimated in round numbers as sixteen thousand millions of dollars; and "it is perfectly safe to assume," says Mr. Horace Greeley, "that fifteen of the sixteen thousand millions of property returned, in 1860, had been created and added to the wealth of the world by the industry, enterprise and thrift of our people, during the eighty preceding years."

These vast figures suffice to measure the growth and greatness of our country—to place the prospect and the retrospect in their proper relations to each other—without descending to that multitude of statistical details, the effect of which is rather to vex and dull the reader than to enlighten and impress him. It is easy to revamp pages of the census into a chapter or article; but such statistical exhibits too often bewilder and distress the mind, instead of making the distinct and deep impression that is desired. Indeed, it is much from this unpleasant treatment of the subject, this burdening it with numbers past recollection, and from excessive repetitions of the theme, that the greatness of America does not impress our people as it should, and sometimes fails of attention, as the *decantatum* of demagogues; although it is, to-day, the standing marvel of all intelligent curiosity in Europe, the phenomenon of the age, the unequaled wonder of modern times, the greatest practical problem of humanity. There is nothing in history like the rapid growth of our country. The greatness of England since the day of the Stuarts, when as Macauldy declared she ascended from a fifth-rate power to the first rank—the most prominent event in the modern history of Europe—is an affair of centuries; while a few decades have served to accomplish the present wonders of American progress. There were men in Europe, a few years ago, who thought or hoped the greatness of America would expire or much diminish in the convulsions of the recent war; but the very revelations of our greatness which that war has made, not only to the world but to ourselves, will yet prove morally more valuable than all that has been lost or ravaged in the collisions of our arms. Those revelations could have been made more powerfully, more conspicuously in no other way; and it is remarkable that there never has been a period of time, or a position of retrospect, wherein the united American people have been more convinced of their greatness, or more awakened to put forth their energies, and make conquests of the future, than when contemplating the displays of the past war, and surveying the monuments of power. which it has left us as new standards and new inspirations of our national life.

One view naturally comes here to the mind, in which the growth and greatness of our country is of sublime and surpassing interest. It is, that in the presence of this mighty picture all mere party controversies fall into insignificance; that it is the vital inspiration of our patriotism, the constant appeal to our loyalty, kindling the best sentiments of the citizen, and associating with his pride his duties to the Government. Every one who dared to read his heart within the past few years must recall how powerful was that argument against the war, which plead the united greatness and glory of the country, and appealed from that alone to the sentiment of patriotism. Almost every nation has its traditional, peculiar appeal by which its patriotism is excited, and its arms summoned to great trials. With us it is traditional only to a limited extent; it is not so much the inspiration coming from names and deeds numbered in distant periods of history, as it is the present visible impression of the greatness of our country, engaging our pride and hopes and curiosity, and inciting the resolution to keep intact the vast magnificent picture so admirable to the world. Its very extent forbids its division or mutilation. It is like a holy unity of art, not to be marred by the substitution of a single part or circumstance. Our patriotism passes into poetry; and as an artist pleads for the very fullness of his conception, the American citizen, aroused and strengthened by a new inspiration, contends for the completeness and integrity, the dramatic unity of the great picture of his country's power and glory.

But there is yet another reflection on this picture, and one we have especially designed in its production to the reader. It is to suggest enlarged solicitude for the future of the Government entrusted with concerns so vast and magnificent; to increase and animate the endeavours of the patriotic to preserve a form of government which has been so beneficent, and which, we shall presently see, is alone competent to deal with such an extent and diversity of interests. In the presence of the picture we have exhibited, we are entering a second great era of American history—the era of Re-union, ensuing after a fierce and terrible war. It is a common disposition of political parties to seize on all eras, all great convulsions in history, and convert them to the purposes of a revolution in their peculiar interest. It is this tendency we have been called upon to resist at the conclusion of the late war; and the great popular care is that this second era of the nation may be a continuation of former peace and prosperity and not a revolutionary succession, hazarding not only the abundant fruits and accumulations of the past, but the future life of the nation.

A revolution as against the peculiar political system of the Union is for the American people far more vital and important than most of the revolutions, of which we have an account in history, such as merely imply the change of a dynasty, or the reform of an administration. We maintain this proposition on the ground that the present government of America with its peculiar distribution of political powers is the only possible one for such an extent of country and such a character of population, and that thus the question of the government and the question of the life of the nation, are, as does not often happen in history, identified, and become one and inseparable.

There is nothing more remarkable in the cotemporary political world than the composite character of the American people. It is perhaps not pleasant to our vanity to recognize how much we are indebted in our elements of progress to the streams of foreign population, which have continued to flow in upon us within the term of our national independence. We recollect a recent estimate, referring to the census of 1860, made in a work of Sir Morton Peto on America, and since adopted in the speech of a United States Senator, that the European emigrants to America and *their descendants*, in the present century, to the date referred to, numbered twenty one million, or about two-thirds of our population in 1860! The singular fact appears from this, that not more than one-third of our population is native, in the sense of being traced to American parentage, since 1800. If we look behind that date, we may go back to the colonial history, and we find a country incongruously settled by Swedes, Dutch, French, Spanish and English. What is remarkable, too, is the want of binding moral influences in a population so mixed. We have none of the harmonizing influence of a uniform spiritual belief. We receive every day enormous bodies of emigrants bringing with them the most various ideas about religion and government. We live under the influences of a constant and reciprocal action between America and Europe, which confuses every attempt at analysis.

In this condition of things it is evident that the problem, for America to solve, is territorial consolidation (not political consolidation). If the ingenuity of man had been taxed for a system of government to suit this extraordinary condition, the invention could not be more exact than the American Union, as devised in 1787, founded on the novel, admirable idea of a confederate unity, standing in some respects for a national identity, a complete territorial consolidation, limited and qualified by the principle of local sovereignty. We can really imagine no other possible accomodation of the incongruous population of America, feeling, as they do, the necessity of a general government for certain purposes, yet having an Anglo-Saxon attachment to their local institutions, and deeply penetrated by a love of individual liberty, than in the Union as formed by our fathers. It is the Union in this interpretation which is now imperiled by the designs of a revolutionary party, and with it all the greatness and growth of America.

"It," says President Johnson, speaking of the Union he defends, "is the best form of government the world ever saw. No other is or can be so well adapted to the genius, habits or wants of the American people. Combining the strength of a great empire with unspeakable blessings of local self-government, having a central power to defend the general interests, and recognizing the authority of the States as the guardians of industrial rights, it is the sheet-anchor of our safety abroad, and our peace at home."

THE TRUE NATURE AND SERVICE OF THE UNION.

The political novelty of the American Union—No mission apart from the States—A curious reflection on political science—Thomas Jefferson's idea of "ward republics" —Political decentralization in America—"The Union as it was," the logical expression of the "Lost Cause"—The Union, as an object of idolatry—Necessity of an element of reverence in our political system—Consolidation more odious than Secession—Power and certainty of public opinion arising out of the nature of the Union—A new value of State institutions—Public opinion, the supreme ruler and the last arbiter.

It is very well known, that preceding that union of the States constructed after the Revolution, there had been a number of other unions or confederations. But these were mere pacts or leagues; they did not contain the distinctive trait and virtue of the union of 1787, in which the world was to see for the first time combined and harmonized the principle of geographical sovereignties with that of a confederation which, for certain purposes, and especially in the regard of foreign powers, was to stand as a distinct, uniform nationality.

The political novelty, the peculiar and fundamental idea of the Union was simple enough. It was the combination of a common chief magistracy with the largest reservation of liberty in its constituents, and the assertion of local institutions as the main depositories of political power. The idea of such a chief magistracy, erected for the national good, controlled by the will of the parties to it, resting on the voluntary basis, strengthened by moral considerations, and severely limited by the principle of local independence, was new to the world, and, as we shall shortly see, was a capital step towards perfection in the science of government.

The reader anxious to comprehend this new political system must bear in mind that the necessity which originated the Union was a necessity for purely economical purposes. The Constitution of the United States, considered in a broad, historical light, was not a revolution, in the sense of a proclamation of a new civil polity; for the civil institutions of the State, as derived from the common law of England, were already perfect and satisfactory, and it is remarkable that they have remained without material change for nearly a century.

The new Union was not a political revolution. It was a convenience of the States, growing out of their wants of a system by which they might have a common agent, and a uniform code on concerns common between themselves. It is in this sense, indeed, that the moral significance of the American Union is interpreted; in this sense its great political virtue was contained. There was put before the eyes of mankind not a consolidated nationality; not a simple republic with an anomalous and indescribable appendage of "States," which are not provinces, or cantons, or territories, and yet, in a sense, subordinate; not some undefined and mis-shapen political mongrel; but a spectacle, such as it had never seen—an association of co-equal and sovereign States, with a common authority, the subjects of which were sufficient to give it the effect of an American and national identity—a government which derived its entire life from the good will, the mutual interests and the unconstrained devotion of the States which at once originated and composed it.

The Union was to be limited by its beneficence to the States. It had no dynastic element; it had no mission apart from the States; it had no independent authority over individuals, except within the scope of the powers delegated to it by the

States. In short, it was a compact which covered only the interests which it specified, yet quite large enough to stand as an American nationality for all practical purposes.

The science of government is fundamentally of the simplest description. The sage who wished his son to attend a great political convention, that he might see what little wisdom it took to govern the world, expressed a profound truth, and not a flippant satire, or a melancholy reflection, as some have interpreted it. When we come to penetrate with an analytic philosophy the most excellent of man's inventions, we discover the invariable condition of extreme simplicity of the fundamental idea, co-existent with a multitude of details enlarging and perfecting the application—the degree of perfection being in proportion to the number and exactness of these details. The progress of all perfection is in details—the intricacy of the superstructure erected on a simple idea. Take, for instance, the steam engine: what more simple than the expansive movement of steam, and the application of leverage to it! But on this principle we find constructed a net-work of machinery, which together becomes more nice and powerful in action, in precise proportion to the number of details, as long as these are properly adjusted.

The two conditions of human invention—simplicity of the fundamental idea and multiplicity of details—are singularly well fulfilled in the political structure of the American Union. We have at the foundation the simple idea of the union of a General Government with State Rights—the union of a common magistracy with reservations of local liberty—and on this idea our true progress in government is to multiply, to adjust, to interlace the relations between the State and the General Government—to produce the greatest possible intricacy without creating confusion. The peculiar task of American statesmanship, its most intelligent and highest mission, is to be constantly adding to, adjusting and refining these relations between the central and local authorities; is to subdivide the political power to the extremest limits; is to multiply as much as possible the local depositories of power. No man better conceived this idea of American statesmanship growing out of the peculiar nature of our government than did Thomas Jefferson. He was for following the principle of local liberty in the State governments to yet further institutions, and subdividing the political power of the country even down to *ward republics.* In a letter to Samuel Kercheval, dated in 1816, proposing certain changes in the Constitution of Virginia he wrote: "These wards, called townships in New England, are the vital principle of their governments, and have proved themselves the wisest invention ever devised by the wit of man for the perfect exercise of self-government and for its preservation. We shall thus marshal our Government into, 1. The general Federal republic, for all concerns foreign and federal; 2. That of the State, for what relates to our own citizens exclusively; 3. The county republics, for the duties and concerns of the county; and 4. The ward republics, for the small and yet numerous and interesting concerns of the neighbourhood: and in governnent, as well as in every other business of life, it is by division and subdivision of duties alone, that all matters, great and small, can be managed to perfection."

Understanding that the true direction of American statesmanship is essentially to political decentralization; that it is a necessity growing out of the very nature of our government, we may better appreciate the extent of aberration of the revolutionary party now governing at Washington. It is to bring our remarks to this point that the foregoing reflections have been designed.

"The Union, as it was," is the true and logical expression of that "Lost Cause" which the country is in prospect of regaining, or on the point of losing forever. It is the most captivating and powerful phrase in which the controversy can be expressed, in behalf of the South, and of the conservative party of the country. We repeat the firm belief, on which we have enlarged in the foregoing pages, that the party of Consolidation stands, at present, in weaker attitude than ever before in the history of the country; because it has attached to it the unpopular and odious particular measure of the elevation of the Negro, at the expense of the constitutional and traditional liberty of the white man in America. But, again, the danger is, that that party has already so progressed in power by increasing ratios, has accumulated so much of influence, that it will be difficult to arrest it on the unpopularity of particular measures. We have, therefore, conceived the necessity, after having discussed in previous parts of this work Consolidation, with reference to its special topics of Reconstruction and Negrophilism, to exhibit the abstract and essential evils of the doctrine, apart from particular questions, and thus complete the argument against the revolutionary movement taking place in our government.

The last and supreme exhibition of the so-called Radical party is that in which it combats the true principle of the Union, and destroys the peculiar and essential sources of American patriotism. Our affections for the Union can only be explained on the grand and august theory of co-equal sovereign States, ennobled by mutual confidences, enthused by common affections, inspired by a single destiny. This is the peculiarity of our political system; this the especial form of our patriotism.

This peculiarity and the affections which attach to it, Consolidation at once destroys. It reduces "the glorious Union" to a mere geographical name; it makes it only the convenient designation of a certain extent of territory, without any particular claims upon our regards. The Union has lost its distinctive moral traits, and the affections which have grown out of them, and which constitute so large an element of American patriotism, perish along with the destruction of the theory of a novel and august combination of equal States. It is this theory which has been beautified by so many illustrations drawn from the stars of the sky, governed by a common centre; the billows, distinct, but "one as the sea;" the noblest and sublimest images of nature. It is this theory which has furnished so many themes of patriotic eloquence; which has so often stirred the popular heart with grand imaginations; in which the orator has found unfailing sources of inspiration; which, indeed, has occupied the most of whatever there is of beauty in the political literature of America.

It is remarkable how this literature has been devoted to the consecration of the Union; how it abounds in paraphrases of it, as a singular object of patriotic adoration. The time was, when no public speaker could obtain admiration, without some tribute to the great and glorious Union. Poets have hymned its praises. The earliest essays of the sophomore, and the maturest efforts of the statesmen, have paid tribute to it, as the supernal work of our political fathers. It has been described as the last, best gift of government to man. Those who made it have been honoured as benefactors, and sometimes invested with a superstitious regard. "They," says President Johnson, "obtained a higher than human wisdom."

The first impulse is to reprove these excesses, to treat them as the rhetorical tumours of the demagogue, a characteristic extravagance of the hustings. This, indeed, is the not unusual criticism of sober and cultivated minds. Why should the Union be apotheosized?—why should it not be spoken of in plain, exact language?—why make it the subject of rhetorical displays? These are the thoughts which first and naturally occur on the singular exaltation of language concerning the Union, so remarkable in our political literature. But a more profound reflection follows these first impressions; and at the end of it, we are not only willing to tolerate what we first deemed a rhetorical extravagance for the Union, but to encourage it as one of the most valuable demonstrations of patriotic sentiment.

The great want of our government is an element of reverence.. The tendency of a harsh and excessive modern democracy is to reduce government to the aspect of a mere affair of police. Such a tendency is essentially revolutionary, productive of changes, in proportion as there are substituted for the fine emotions of patriotism the caprices of selfishness, or the calculations of utility. In every stable government we naturally inquire for some objects of reverential regard, some moral inspiration, some sources of affection through which men love their government, rather than calculate it on a mere system of debits and credits. We are profoundly convinced that patriotism must be sentimental to a degree, to be true patriotism. The tendency in America, sometimes encouraged by a most false and superficial statesmanship, is to divest the government too much of sacred and reverential regards. The processes of utilitarianism, excellent as they may be within certain limits, must be arrested before the government becomes, in popular estimation, a mere institution of police, a mere convenience of public order. In America, the limited extent and influence of our traditions, the absolute divorce of the Church from the State, the common denudation of the ceremonials and insignia of authority, have brought the country to a condition where the thoughtful and philosophic mind perceives the necessity of some element of reverence in the government, to sustain it in the affections of the people, and to inspire a patriotism above the mean and changeful regards of selfishness.

It is in this sense that we find the supreme value of a veneration for the Union—the supply of a great and growing want in the moral economy of the American system of government. The patriotism of every country must have some great rallying cry. As we have elsewhere said, we have such, to a certain extent, in the names of our political ancestors, in limited traditions. But we would add to this appeal "the Union"—as something peculiarly glorious and sacred; picturing, as nothing else can, the greatness of our country; sanctified as the first fruits of the blood of the Revolution of 76, revered even as the product of a wisdom "higher than human."

There may be an extravagance in these appeals, when brought to severe tests of logic; but no nation is expected to measure its patriotic memories by the cold and exact rules of history.

We have traced the swift and decisive steps which Consolidation has taken since the war. We have followed them, in preceding pages, almost to the destruction of the Union. We have seen the establishment of military rule and Negro domination in the South; the attempt to clench this ruinous policy on so large a part of the country, by requiring that the re-admitted State shall never change the organic laws under which it is admitted—a satire and mockery of "republicanism"—by prostituting the Supreme court, and compelling it to assume the constitutionality of all the acts of Reconstruction, and, at last, by attacking the Executive office, and attempting to reduce it to a condition of absolute servility to Congress.

It is well that this last proceeding should be understood as part of this general design, rather than as a mere personal episode in the history of an Administration; and that the country should perceive that it was not Andrew Johnson alone, who lately stood at the bar of the Senate of the United States, but that the great body of American liberties was arraigned there, and the tutelar genius of the Constitution insulted and disrobed in the presence of a shallow and tittering curiosity.

Against the progress of Consolidation, advancing to the overthrow of the government and the verge of destruction, we have urged various appeals, not one of which is exaggerated. We have appealed to the interests of our civilization; to community of race; to whatever is dear in the past, or hopeful in the future. The last appeal we put up is *the Union*—that for which the war was fought, and which for three generations has symbolized our greatness, and assured our prosperity.

The Union may be more effectually destroyed by Consolidation than by Secession. The first is far more odious, and especially in the present instance, with the stripe of Negro government in it. Far better that the States should disband into petty republics still preserving their institutions of local government, than pass into an imperial despotism, disfigured, too, by Negro rule. It is thus that the revolutionary design of Congress, in every logical respect, exceeds whatever was claimed of evil for the "rebellion" of 1861, and forces the country to an issue, of which the past war was only a partial and imperfect exposition. The imminent danger is that the country has, indeed, been brought to a condition, where there is no longer a remedy in the political structure itself, where its checks and balances no longer operate, as they were designed in the Constitution; and where the only resource is outside of it, in the mass of the people.

It is said that the people, in all parts of the country, are gloomy and impassive. There is, indeed, a popular tameness which is the forerunner of easy and successful despotism, when the people manifestly quit their interest in political affairs, and the mass becomes an unresisting prey to whatever government alights upon it. But this, we firmly believe, is not the true interpretation of whatever quiet there may be in the country outside of the circle at Washington. There is a quiet which comes from the consciousness of strength; from the assurance of a last, supreme, certain resort; from the confidence of perfect ability to restore what has been lost, and to appoint its own times and opportunities of action.

This perfect ability yet resides in our people; and the opportunities of action are yet abundant. The people are still able to act, having not yet been actually fettered; and the condition is one upon which public opinion may operate with unlimited effect.

We do not know that it has ever been observed what rare and remarkable power public opinion has in America, arising from the peculiar nature of the Union. We claim it as the discovery of a new virtue in our political system. It is the essential design of Consolidation and Imperialism to keep public opinion diffuse and disorganized, to destroy all its centres and rallying points, and thus to render it measurably incapable of action. In America, the value of our State institutions is, that they maintain vast bodies of public opinion ready and organized at any moment to oppose the usurpations of the general government. It is an inestimable service; and it is surprising that so many commentators on the Union have failed to perceive this greatest of its virtues, in keeping large and independent organizations of public opinion in the State Governments, that can be summoned at any time into operation, having their own machinery, their own agents, their own military establishments. It is thus, through the very nature of the Union, that we have been so busy to describe, that public opinion in America has a certainty and power which it has nowhere else in the world. In European countries, the sentiment of the people is seldom ascertained; it is never known; it is a vague and diffuse thing, at best; and the statesman who asserts it is listened to as scarcely more than the utterer of a rhetorical platitude, incapable of proof. But in our country, and especially through the State Government, public opinion may not only be more certainly known, but it is a power, constantly erect, perfectly organized, that can be summoned at all times to swift and decisive issues.

It is this public opinion, already organized and alert in all the States—except those ridden by military rule—and growing out of the very nature of the Union which it is invoked to protect, that indicates the true hope of the country, and contains all lost causes of constitutional liberty. All recommendations to force are hasty and unnecessary, in view of the extraordinary powers of this opinion; and there are no grounds of comparison with revolutionary appeals in other countries.

The American political system is yet competent to right itself, without the violence of arms. The "Lost Cause" needs no war to regain it. We have taken up new hopes, new arms, new methods—

> "By winning words to conquer willing hearts,
> And make persuasion do the work of fear."

THE END.

Mrs. Mary J. Holmes' Works.

'LENA RIVERS.—	A novel.	12mo. cloth,	$1.50
DARKNESS AND DAYLIGHT.—	do.	do.	$1.50
TEMPEST AND SUNSHINE.—	do.	do.	$1.50
MARIAN GREY.—	do.	do.	$1.50
MEADOW BROOK.—	do.	do.	$1.50
ENGLISH ORPHANS.—	do.	do.	$1.50
DORA DEANE.—	do.	do.	$1.50
COUSIN MAUDE.—	do.	do.	$1.50
HOMESTEAD ON THE HILLSIDE.—	do.	do.	$1.50
HUGH WORTHINGTON.—	do.	do.	$1.50
THE CAMERON PRIDE.—*Just Published.*		do.	$1.50

Artemus Ward.

HIS BOOK.—The first collection of humorous writings by A. Ward. Full of comic illustrations. 12mo. cloth, $1.50

HIS TRAVELS.—A comic volume of Indian and Mormon adventures. With laughable illustrations. 12mo. cloth, $1.50

IN LONDON.—A new book containing Ward's comic *Punch* letters, and other papers. Illustrated. 12mo. cloth, $1.50

Miss Augusta J. Evans.

BEULAH.—A novel of great power.		12mo. cloth,	$1.75
MACARIA.—	do. do.	do.	$1.75
ST. ELMO.—	do. do. *Just published.*	do.	$2.00

By the Author of "Rutledge."

RUTLEDGE.—A deeply interesting novel.		12mo. cloth,	$1.75
THE SUTHERLANDS.—	do.	do.	$1.75
FRANK WARRINGTON.—	do.	do.	$1.75
ST. PHILIP'S.—	do.	do.	$1.75
LOUIE'S LAST TERM AT ST. MARY'S.—		do.	$1.75
ROUNDHEARTS AND OTHER STORIES.—For children.		do.	$1.75
A ROSARY FOR LENT.—Devotional readings.		do.	$1.75

J. Cordy Jeaffreson.

A BOOK ABOUT LAWYERS.—Reprinted from the late English Edition. Intensely interesting. 12mo. cloth, $2.00

Allan Grant.

LOVE IN LETTERS.—A fascinating book of love-letters from celebrated and notorious persons. 12mo. cloth, $2.00

Algernon Charles Swinburne.

LAUS VENERIS—and other Poems and Ballads. 12mo. cloth, $1.75

Geo. W. Carleton.

OUR ARTIST IN CUBA.—A humorous volume of travel; with fifty comic illustrations by the author. 12mo. cloth, $1.50

OUR ARTIST IN PERU.— do. do. $1.50

www.ingramcontent.com/pod-product-compliance
Lightning Source LLC
LaVergne TN
LVHW011210110826
845150LV00006B/1388

9781425518196